The Gardener's
Christmas Book

THE GARDENER'S CHRISTMAS BOOK

The Art of Decorating for Christmas

by Helen Snow Wilson Goddard

PHOTOGRAPHS BY PAUL GENEREUX

WOOD SCULPTURE BY CARL GODDARD

THE MACMILLAN COMPANY, NEW YORK

COLLIER-MACMILLAN LTD., LONDON

Library of Congress Catalog Card Number: 67-26639

The Macmillan Company, New York
Collier-Macmillan Canada Ltd., Toronto, Ontario
Printed in the United States of America

CONTENTS

The Gardener's
Christmas Book

INTRODUCTION

ALTHOUGH all the decorations in this book were primarily designed in sizes and colors to fit my own home, my hope is that they will inspire readers of this book to create their own decorations in their own colors and combinations of materials. If you wish to copy them exactly as shown, this book can be a comprehensive guide, but sometimes, all that is needed is a thought or an inspiration in order to get started. A suggestion of how to begin can often be sufficient to ignite the creative spark.

The sequence followed in the book begins with the garden gate, proceeds to the front door, and continues into the house. We have two living rooms: one is slightly formal, the other is more casual. The casual one, or family room, has come to be called the Chestnut Room, and we live and work in it most of the time. The decorations for these two rooms have been separated and appear under different titles. However, it is not necessary to consider the formal and casual division as a strict one. For instance, many of the wreaths that are used in the family room would very easily fit into a more formal living room by merely changing the backgrounds and accessories.

The joyousness of Christmas time can pervade your

entire home and its festive gaiety be felt in every room. When decorating, be bold, creative, and experimental. Let the basic principles and suggestions in this book help you to that time when you will happily improvise your own creations.

There is no doubt that my predominant use of natural materials stems from my experience with and love of gardening. For me, nothing can replace such materials. In their warm and living earthiness there is, for me, the spirit of Christmas, which is peace; the gladness of Christmas, which is hope; and the heart of Christmas, which is love.

Christmas is a most exciting time of year for those of us who like to decorate because of the great variety of decorations you can make yourself. There are the simple, old-fashioned decorations, the gay ones for young children. There are nut-and-cone decorations, the modern glittery ones, the quiet religious things, and finally the ones I love the most—those made of fruits and flowers.

The choice is so wide, perhaps your head whirls with thoughts, "What shall I make?" "How shall I make it?" How often have I heard people say, "I just can't do anything with my hands." So, let me inject a thought right here.

It is not your *hands*—it is your *head*. Your hands will do anything your head tells them to do. In this book, you are told in the simplest, easiest way possible exactly how to make the decorations pictured here. After your initial success with some of these, you will undoubtedly want to attempt some of your own inspiration.

There are many spots to decorate at Christmas time. Front doors and mantels are traditional places, of course, but have you considered the inside of the front door? This can be a very interesting location because it is so prominent. Then there is the kitchen, the bedrooms, and even the bathroom door. And have you considered taking down pictures and mirrors to create wall space? This will often change the feeling of the whole room and provide adequate space for some stunning decorations. One or two shelves removed from a bookcase can make a shadowbox or niche. And let us not forget the garden!

I feel it does not matter what you combine to make your creations so long as they harmonize in size, color, and texture.

Be sure to relate the size of the arrangement to other things. In order to achieve an arrangement of appropriate size for a particular room, you will have to consider the space from the floor to the ceiling, the area of the room itself, the furnishings in the room, and the accessories. For outdoor decorations similar factors have to be taken into account. For example, the size of the wreath used on your front door is governed not only by the size of the door but also the distance your house is set back from the street. A 12-inch wreath made up of small forms is fine if the house is near the sidewalk. If the house is some distance from the street, then a larger wreath made up of larger forms is more impressive and effective. The greater the distance from which a wreath is seen, the larger it should be, though naturally you must also take into consideration the size of the house itself.

Color choice today is almost unlimited. There was a time when monochromatic, analagous, or complementary color schemes were the only ones used. But today with the acceptance of modern art, anything seems to go. I myself still prefer rich quiet colors. However, this is a matter of personal choice. Whether we are consciously aware of it or not, color has a strong effect on us. It excites, stimulates, disturbs, upsets, pleases, calms, refreshes, relaxes, cools, and warms. Surround yourself with the colors that please you. That will make your decorations individual and personal.

Many times color is the most important part of a decoration. The design may be extremely simple but the color combinations can make the decoration outstanding and distinctive. We all know that dark colors seem heavier and tend to recede, while light colors advance, so keep these facts in mind. Also be aware of the amount of light there will be on a completed decoration. Purple is one of my favorite colors but I have to be careful to use it in a well lighted spot or it will be completely lost. The use of purple at Christmas when combined with red or blue-green is most effective and to me accents the religious feeling that should be a part of our Christmas joy.

Light colors give highlights and airiness. Strong, brilliant, intense colors are well suited to contemporary houses and designs, but these can also be used in houses of other periods. Don't be afraid of color; experiment and have fun with it.

Texture is a thing you can see and almost feel just by looking at it. Materials with different textures create strikingly different effects—for example, velvet compared to burlap; glass grapes to real grapes; artificial evergreen roping to natural evergreen roping. They all have their own textural feeling, which must be considered when they are to be combined with other materials.

Texture can change the entire feeling of an arrangement. A rough burlap surface covering an area will absorb light, giving an entirely different mood than would a piece of silk with its smoother texture and high sheen.

Many odd and unusual things can be combined to create effective decorations. Even though it might seem that there is nothing new in the world, what can be new is the combination of materials that you choose. No matter what the combination may be, as long as the elements go together in size, color, and texture, your design will be good.

Many bases, parts, or units of a decoration can be made so that they are usable year after year. I have decorations that I have displayed over and over again, but each year in a different way with a different combination of materials and in different parts of the house. In the pictures to follow, you will see some of the same decorations used in a number of different ways. It is most interesting to see how the entire feeling of a decoration can be changed by what is combined with it. It almost becomes a yearly game.

Three Basic Types of Wreaths

1. One basic wreath begins with a flat frame of thick, stiff wire. You can purchase this kind of frame at any of the better florist shops. It consists of two rings, one within the other, held in position by a number of wire cross pieces that pass from the large outside ring to the

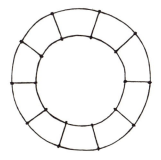

smaller inside ring. These frames come in various sizes;
I use mostly 12-inch and 16-inch frames. The 16-inch
makes a perfect background for the 12-inch frame when
I am making two wreaths to hang together. If the larger
frame is used to make a background wreath, it may simply be wound with ribbon, velvet, or any other kind of
material that suits your design and color scheme.

These flat wire frames may also be used as a base for
beautiful natural greens. To prepare one, you first go to
that bottom bureau drawer, usually in the guest room,
where you keep those odds and ends of fabric which you
were going to use some day. This is the day. Any strong
cotton cloth in a dark color will do—green or brown is
best. Cut the material on the straight of the goods in
strips about 1½ inches wide. It will take 3 yards of
strips for a 12-inch frame, 5 yards for a 16-inch frame.

Starting anywhere on the outer edge of the frame,
simply sew (overcast) or, if you wish, just pin securely
one end of the strip of material to the frame. Then, wind
the strips over the outer and inner rings, overlapping
each time about ½-inch. Wind gently but firmly, so that
it is neither very tight nor loose and floppy—merely firm.
Then, sew or pin the end to finish it off.

The wrappings have created pockets into which you
can tuck short, small pieces of evergreen. Don't make the
mistake of thinking you will make your wreath more
quickly by using large pieces of evergreens— it just doesn't
work that way. Use from three to five pieces, about 4
inches long, in each pocket (or as many as are needed to
make a good full wreath). Almost any kind of evergreen
will do, but my favorites for this type of wreath are yew,
cedar, or white pine. If you have a garden, you can prune
your evergreens now, so that you can use the clippings.
I usually try to save some of my pruning of evergreens

until Christmas time.* I have never found it to harm the shrubs, and it is wonderful to be able to pick them in abundance. Or perhaps you can obtain greens by helping a friend or neighbor at this time. If you have no garden, or are unwilling to prune your evergreens, you can buy bundles of boughs and cut them into short pieces to make your wreaths.

If you have never made a wreath this way, you will be surprised at how quick and simple it is. The base of course is permanent. After Christmas, when the greens have faded, remove them from the pockets, and save the wrapped frame for use again next year. If the needles, although faded, have not dropped, the wreath may be put away as it is for the next year when a coat of gold or silver spray will give it life again. I have a white pine wreath sprayed gold that I have used for nine years. It has acquired a soft mellow patina and is especially charming when used with antiques.

2. The base of the second wreath is a single, crinkled wire frame, available at better florists'. These frames must always be wrapped with florist's tape before you start to make a wreath so that the materials you bind to it will hold firmly. Your choice of materials for this type of wreath is almost unlimited. All kinds of needled and broadleaved evergreens, as well as dried materials, may be used. A few of my favorite dried plants are dock (a weed), pepper weed, corn tips, and wild evening primrose.

---

* Because it is on the conservation list, I should like to emphasize that all the princess pine shown in the photographs came from private property. It was carefully gathered so as not to risk decimating the plant. Princess pine is a joy to use, because it never drops its greenery and dries beautifully, but for those who have no private property to gather from, we suggest using cedar as a replacement.

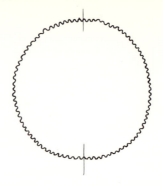

To make an even, round wreath, take three or four pieces of greens or dried materials 3 or 4 inches in length. Wrap these together by twisting a long piece of fine wire around them once and pulling the wire tight. I use 12-inch lengths of 30-gauge wire. Then, place the bunch on the frame and anchor firmly in place by twisting the balance of the wire tightly around the frame. Make another bunch. Place on the frame, overlapping the first one-half its length and wiring it securely in place. Continue around the frame in this manner until the circle is finished. When completed, all the greens will face in the same direction.

Other ways of laying the material in place produce different effects. For example, let us use the same frame in the following manner:

Measure and mark the middle of the top and bottom of the frame. Work on one side at a time, from the middle of the top to the middle of the bottom. Start at the top, wiring on small bunches consisting of only one or two pieces of material. Gradually increase the size of the bunches as you progress, until you reach the middle of the bottom. Repeat on the other half. Achieve an even balance by making sure bunches are approximately the same size, and progress evenly from small to large.

3. The third basic wreath is made of a styrofoam circle. These circles can be obtained at five-and-ten-cent stores and are available in several thicknesses, diameters, and colors. For my own use, I prefer the dark green color in the 1½-inch thickness which I back with cardboard to give increased strength when I am attaching heavy material.

I have found that using a styrofoam base is the easiest, quickest way of making wreaths out of nuts, cones, and

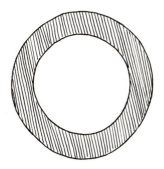

berries; all you need is Elmer's glue and patience. After you have decided on your pattern and have the material ready for gluing, make a bed or pocket for each piece by forcing or pushing the material into the surface of the styrofoam. Don't be afraid to push quite hard. An indentation must be made in the styrofoam to hold the nut, cone, or berry in place. After the bed is made, lift the material out and apply glue to the bed. Not too much, not too little, but just enough to hold. Now, force the material back into its bed. A little experience will quickly teach you how much glue to use.

Be sure not to set all nuts and cones standing up straight like soldiers. Instead lay them on their sides at an angle, in order to achieve a sculptured look when finished. Large pieces or long cones may need to be temporarily held in place with fine wire overnight because, due to their springy nature, they cannot be forced deeply enough into the styrofoam. Lay the wire over the top of the cone and around the wreath. Twist it up tight in back. Long cones may need wiring at both ends. Remove the wire the next day. Caution: Don't try to cover the entire wreath in one day, but do a section at a time, allowing it to dry overnight.

After the styrofoam is covered with large materials as completely as possible, glue smaller cones, berries, and other smaller forms into the interstices between the larger forms. This will give a real third dimension and fill up all the spaces.

At Christmas time, five-and-ten-cent stores carry a wide variety of other shapes cut from styrofoam, such as Christmas trees, bells, stars, and already wired snowballs. You can also buy large blocks of styrofoam and cut your own shapes if you prefer. A sharp butcher knife cuts this material easily and cleanly.

Roping

To make roping, you use the same method employed in making the single crinkled-frame wreath, except that you wire the materials to a length of rope. Old-fashioned clothesline is fine. Cut it to the length you wish. Bunch four or five pieces of greens cut about 3 or 4 inches long. Wrap these together with fine wire, #30 gauge, and fasten to the rope. Continue making the bunches and wiring them on, overlapping them each time about one-half their length, until the rope is fully covered. This will make a thin, flexible roping.

For a heavier roping, you can apply the bunches of greens to the rope in a different manner. Following the sketch, you lay the first bunch lengthwise along the rope (1), then place the next two bunches to the right and the left at an angle to the rope (2 and 3). These bunches should be laid so closely that when repeated along the entire length, they form a thick continuous roping.

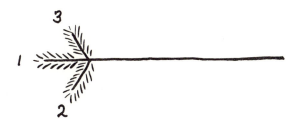

The most difficult part of making roping lies in keeping the rope taut while you work. If you can't find someone who is willing to hold one end while you work toward the other, tie one end to a door knob, but lock the door first!

Roping is perfect for decorating newel posts or banisters of staircases. Ribbon twined around the roping is effective. Also clusters of pine cones or berries can be added for variety.

Arch with a Drop

Another interesting form to display on your front door, over a mantel, or on any other wall space you choose is the arch with a drop. You make the arch by bending a wire coat hanger as indicated in the sketch and wiring

*Bent to arch
ready for greens
to be wired on*

greens to it. Before you wire the greens, bind the coat hanger with florist's tape so that the wires will not slip. Use fine wire (#30 gauge) for delicate materials such as boxwood; heavy spool wire (#24 gauge) for heavy materials such as blue spruce.

You make the drop separately and hang it from the center. It may be a string of pine cones, a child's drum and trumpets, pepper berries, sleigh bells, or something as simple as two drops of ribbon with various-sized Christmas baubles attached. Purple ribbon with blue-green baubles makes a lovely drop to harmonize with a blue spruce arch.

Garlands

Garlands are formed in the same way as roping, except that for roping the greens all face in the same direction, while a garland is divided roughly into quarters that have greens facing in opposite directions (see sketch).

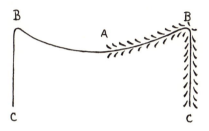

First cut your rope the length you want for the space to be filled. Twist a piece of wire to mark the middle (A); similarly mark with wire the points at which the garland is to be hung, (B); with the vertical drops ending at C. Work from C to B. Then, work from A to B (see instructions for roping), first on one side, and then on the other to keep both balanced. Almost any kind of greens can be used for garlands—pine, spruce, yew, cedar. You can use one kind of material or a mixture.

Other types of garlands using cones, berries, or fruits can be made on styrofoam secured with Elmer's glue by the method described for the third wreath. A garland can also be made on pegboard cut to shape. First, twist wire about each of the materials or bunches of them, then fasten them to the pegboard with the wires. Or, you can make a garland on plywood, Masonite, or hardboard cut to shape and covered by a piece of chicken wire or ½-inch mesh hardware cloth stapled to it. It is a simple matter to tuck in the berries or greens or other materials you wish to use.

Nuts and Cones

There is a wide variety of nuts, cones, seeds, and seed pods to choose from, and working with them can be quite exciting. I like to combine some weathered old gray ones with new ones of light or dark brown.

You can make flower forms out of cones by cutting them in half. To cut smaller cones into flower forms, use your small pruning shears, or wire cutters. Last year's or older cones will cut more easily because they are partly dried. Start cutting just below the middle. With the tip of your shears keep nibbling away until you have cut through the center of the cone. Then, taking either the top or the bottom, you can cut the scales to make whatever kind of flower form you wish. An example of these flowers is shown in the Heritage wreath on page 140.

Long, slender, and large cones can be cut lengthwise with an axe, if you are fairly expert. Be careful, however, as some of these larger cones have a lot of spring in them, and a bouncing axe can be dangerous. Actually, a band saw in the hands of a willing husband or good handyman is your best bet!

Some people prefer to finish a nut-and-cone piece with varnish, but to me, and to many other gardeners, the natural finish is much more pleasing.

Kissing Ball

A kissing ball is a sphere of evergreens, fruits, and sometimes flowers with a cluster of mistletoe suspended from it. There are many varieties of kissing balls. But the one I like best has a potato for its base. Select the roundest potato you can find.

Using a long length of heavy wire, pierce directly through the middle of the potato. Pull the wire through the potato until it projects through about 1 inch or so. Curve this projection into a hook and push the end back into the potato to hold the wire in place. This will be the bottom. The long length of wire projecting from the top is used to hang it; you will usually want to cover this with ribbon.

Cut the sprigs of greens (boxwood, cedar, and yew are best) about 3 inches long and with sharp points on the ends, stick them into the potato quite close together. The moisture in the potato will keep the greens fresh for a long time. Add a sprig of mistletoe at the bottom, making sure that it extends slightly beyond the greens.

Containers and Bases

Containers and bases play a very important part in the over-all design of some decorations. Bases may be especially important, since many containers do not have enough weight at the bottom to balance what is put into them. This does not mean you must obtain an expensive teakwood stand; you will find many interesting and inexpensive things can be used as bases. Look for something unusual that can be adapted. For instance, one of my favorite containers is a solid brass electric light fixture, shown on page 88. Go around your home looking for adaptable objects; turn things upside down and look at them that way. Some things make splendid bases when inverted.

Never pass up an opportunity to buy a *pair* of anything that can be converted into containers. Sometimes one can be turned upside down and the other placed on top of it, making a fine container with a base.

Consider, too, using a flat wire wreath frame wrapped with ribbon or velvet for a base to give weight and color which might otherwise be hard to achieve.

Accessories

Accessories, whether merely a simple candle or a beautiful hand-carved madonna, must be considered part of the whole design. Speaking of hand carving, I wish to mention that all of the carved pieces shown in this book were carved by my husband. Of course there are many other objects of decorative value that can be used in designs.

Sometimes accessories are the beginning of a decoration. For instance, if you have a large object you wish to feature on a table or mantel, start with it and design all the other decorations to balance and contrast or blend with the central object. Accessories are often found in antique shops, secondhand stores, thrift shops, and at rummage sales. Auctions are also a good source, especially church auctions. The lovely antique clock frame shown in this book a number of times was purchased at such an auction. The lady sitting beside me bought a carton full of "stuff" for 50 cents, and protruding from the top of the carton was the clock frame. I offered her 50 cents for just that. She was delighted and so was I, for it has become one of my pets for Christmas decorations.

Lighting

The only decorative lighting used in our house at night is a single white electric candle in each window. For exterior lighting, we use the garden floodlights, which are permanent, plus one extra to accent the front door. I take care to conceal these floodlights and try to place them at such an angle that they do not suddenly blind someone approaching or looking toward them.

Mechanics

The mechanics are the hidden elements which we use to hold our decorations together.

Available at most florist shops and garden centers:

Fine wire (#30 gauge) to use two ways—(1), on the spool when a long continuous length of wire is required, as for evergreen roping, or (2), cut into 12-inch or other lengths for wiring material onto wreaths, etc.

Heavy wire (#24 gauge) on a spool

Pin holders, to support flowers and branches

Florist's clay, to secure holders

Corsage-size aqua picks, for holding small bunches of leaves or flowers in fruit arrangements

Wreath frames—flat wire and crinkled

Available at most five-and-ten-cent stores, hardware stores:

Styrofoam frames and blocks

Glue—Elmer's glue is my usual choice, but there are many other adhesives that will attach nuts, cones, and so forth to styrofoam, plywood, masonite, or whatever background material you choose. Some people use Webtex, a linoleum cement, with great success. Fast-drying Craft adhesive is another all-purpose cement; it dries clear. Thermogrip is one of the newest and quickest-drying glues. It is a white glue which is heated in and then applied by the Thermogrip electric glue gun. It bonds immediately.

Toothpicks—round, heavy

Rope—old-fashioned clothesline for roping and drops

Available at lumber yards or hardware stores:

Pegboard

Plywood

Masonite

Chicken wire

Tools—Pruning shears, wire cutters (also often available at florist shops), saws, scissors, awls, pincers.

A note about conditioning: To condition fresh greens or flowers, pick them early in the morning or late at night. At this time the plant is holding more water than when the sun is shining on it. Plunge the stems into a bucket full of water, keep in a cool dark place overnight.

CHAPTER ONE

OUTDOOR DECORATIONS

BASKET ON GATE WITH FRUIT

A BASKET on a gate gives a cheery welcome not only at Christmas, but the year around. Our basket's original tin liner is replaced each spring with large-size fruit juice cans, which are wide enough and deep enough to hold long stems. A half a brick or a large stone placed at the bottom keeps the basket from tipping if the branches are long and heavy. Our gate itself plus all of the doors, shutters, and other gates are painted purple, exactly the deep color of violets. While the doors and gates are painted a solid color, the shutters are antiqued, with a faded blue showing through the purple.

The photograph shows the gate basket filled with holly and a few sprays of yew, with long drooping sprays of pepper berries arching over the basket, green grapes nestled in the center, and large crabapples placed here and there.

Holly has come to be a symbol of Christmas, but because it dries so quickly in the house, I find that it is much better to use holly out-of-doors.

The grapes were enjoyed by the birds and had to be replaced occasionally.

CRABAPPLE AND PEPPER BERRY
WREATH AND SWAGS

The combination of these three matching decorations makes a complete and unusual trimming for the front door.

Long sprays of yew make a background for the swags. Make sure to use one or two short sprays at the top for a finish. Using heavy wire, attach tips of hemlock that are abundant with cones. (Our sprays were fresh last year and so by now had dropped all their needles, but the cones had remained on the branches. Against the background of yew, the needles of the hemlock were not missed at all.) With fine wire, next attach bunches of pepper berries and finally clusters of green crabapples. Wire each apple separately, piercing it through the center just beside the core with heavy wire. Twist the two ends of the wire together to make a false stem. Make clusters of these apples by twisting the false stems together, then wire them to the swag. White pine cones finish the swag; use one on each side of the apple clusters.

There are actually two wreaths on the door: One is a 16-inch flat wire frame filled with white pine, which frames the other—a 12-inch flat wire frame filled with yew and decorated with fruits and flowers. It is much more effective to use two separate wreaths in this manner than to simply make a 16-inch Della Robbia wreath. It is

more work, but I feel it is worth it. You create an interesting texture and color effect by the use of the two evergreens. The white pine is light and airy, while the yew is rich in color and makes a dense, more compact wreath.

The materials we use for the Della Robbia wreath (see page 136) are crabapples, kumquats, yellow strawflowers, small yellow crabapples, blue starflowers, and pepper berries.

BASKET ON GATE WITH WHEAT

Yew is the main green used in this arrangement, with a few sprigs of *Leucothoe Catesbaei* to add variety. If you are not familiar with this shrub, it is a rather open growing plant with fine white flowers borne in spring on long pendulous racemes. The leaves are glossy green in summer but take on a purplish red tint in late fall. It is one of the best long-lasting broadleaf evergreens for arranging that I know of. It blends beautifully with the purplish-red of the pepper berries that hang so gracefully over the front of the basket. It likes a shady spot and sour soil to grow in, by the way.

A few golden sprays of natural wheat tucked in top of the basket tie in with the wheat sheaf on the door. Wheat may seem delicate and rather fragile, but it will actually stand up to bad weather, even heavy snow. Stored carefully, it will last from year to year and keep quite fresh looking unless you happen to have a few field mice living with you. However, by wrapping these wheat stalks in foil paper and adding a handful of mothballs, it should be safe.

WHEAT AND BELLS ON DOOR

Here, an antique gold clock frame was wired to the door knocker to be used as a background for the imposing sheaf of wheat. First the wheat was tied together near the heads, then fanned out to make a widespread base. Norway spruce cones were wired together in a circle, then wired to the wheat. Clusters of glass baubles of graduated sizes in shades from gold to yellow-green fall from the middle of the circle of cones. (The larger balls are gold.)

This decoration, like many shown in this book, is a combination of Old World and modern—the glass baubles are modern, the clock antique. The gold-to-green shading of the baubles blends the composition together.

The antique gold clock frame will appear a number

of times in this book, illustrating how a single good piece has many, many uses. It is a favorite of mine because it seems to simulate the radiation of light. I find it harmonizes with very simple things as well as more elaborate ones.

The bells at the top of the door are old electric light fixtures turned upside down. Made of solid brass, they can be polished to a beautiful luster. Such fixtures are found in junk shops or attics, or may be obtained from an electrician who does rewiring. We inserted a cork stopper in the top of each and set a screw eye into this to afford a means of wiring the bells together and hanging them. A cluster of small gold glass baubles, their own stems twisted together and stuck into the cork, make the clappers. I have never found lovelier shaped bells than these.

PEPPER BERRY SWAG ON GATE

On our gate we usually hang a basket of fruit, flowers, and greens at Christmas time, but one year the red spruce cones were so full and so abundant they suggested a

swag for this spot. Because we planned to use pepper berries on the door, we wired bunches of these berries to a cone-covered red spruce branch in order to carry out the color scheme. I find pepper berries perfect to use in spots where you want to use red for Christmas but where a true red is too strong, too bright, or too heavy. Their color, a blend of pink and red, is complementary to all shades of greens and blues and is most delightful with purple. The clusters of pepper berries seem to entwine and intermingle with whatever they are combined with which gives them support and holds them together. They appear to be delicate but are really quite rugged.

Pepper berries grow in California and are usually on the market at better florists' around Thanksgiving. It is wise to purchase them when they are first available; otherwise you may find them in short supply near Christmas. The stems are extremely fine. For this reason, use only fine wire—#30 gauge.

GARLAND ON DOOR USING
PEPPER BERRIES

Both Masonite and plywood are suitable materials for making the background frame for this garland. It can be cut into the proper shape either with a power jig saw, or a fine-toothed handsaw. You then cover the frame with small-size chicken wire about 2 inches larger than the frame in all directions, then fold it over the edge all the way around and staple or tack it to the back. Make sure to leave the chicken wire a bit loose, to allow for tucking in the pepper berries.

Make small bunches of pepper berries. Cut the stems

about 2 or 3 inches long and, using fine #30 wire, bind them together. Tuck the bunches into the chicken wire. On each dropped side, work from the bottom to the top overlapping the bunches of berries and thus covering the stems. Next work from the center of the middle swag upward to the outside points, alternately, first on one side and then on the other (see page 13). For the last few bunches at the top of the corners, cut the stems very short. The magnolia leaves and white pine will cover any stems that may still show. Fine hair nets covering the berries will give good protection from strong winter winds.

Real pink poinsettias in a terra cotta pot on the step will complement the pepper berries during the day if it is a warm Christmas or where the climate permits.

Center of Middle Swag

First cut a Scotch pine cone in flower form. To make the star, wire five Norway spruce cones and the Scotch pine cone separately, using #30 wire and leaving about 3 inches of wire extending from each cone. Place the Scotch pine in the center of the spruce cones. Holding the six wires in one hand, twist the wired cones with your other hand until they come together to form a star.

Wind the garland with yellow-green satin ribbon. Next, wire on the magnolia leaves, then the star and cones, and lastly tuck in the white pine.

Swags on Shutters

The falls on the shutters are the same as the pepper berry swag on the gate on page 27, except that they were hung vertically and fewer pepper berries were used. White pine and magnolia leaves give a flair and a finish at the top.

By replacing the evergreens, you can make this decoration last for many years. If the berries fade, you may spray-paint it any of a number of colors. My suggestion for storing any decoration made with pepper berries is to wrap it in foil paper, adding a handful of mothballs before closing to protect it from rodents. The rattle of the paper frightens the mice, and the odor of the mothballs is unpleasant to them.

EUONYMUS BERRY AND KUMQUAT
WREATH ON DOOR

One year the berries on our euonymus were so abundant
I couldn't resist making a wreath of them. As a base I
used a 12-inch crinkly wire frame wrapped first with tape.
Taking bunches of berries about 3 inches in length, I
wired them together with fine wire, then wired them to
the frame with each bunch overlapping the previous one
about half way. Next I wired on clusters of kumquats
with their own foliage still attached.

Then I wrapped a 16-inch flat wire frame with cloth and filled it with white pine, cutting pieces to about 4 inches long and tucking five or six into each pocket to make a full and abundant wreath. The two wreaths were then wired together and hung on the door under a carved wood arch.

The brass bells hanging in the center of the wreath and the three bells below, attached to the brass door knocker, came from different countries.

If you don't have on hand an abundance of euonymus berries, bittersweet would make an excellent substitute.

GARLAND OR SWAG ON DOOR

This garland or swag (call it whichever you choose) might at first glance appear to be difficult to make. Actually, it makes up very quickly and easily, for most of the materials used are large forms.

First, cut a large piece of styrofoam to crescent shape, in the size that will fit your space. Next cut a piece of cardboard the same shape and glue it to the back of the styrofoam to give added stiffness. Assemble all the materials to be used: large Southern and Italian pine cones cut into flower forms, Norway spruce and Scotch pine cones, oak balls, pignuts, acorns, wild cucumbers, fernleaf yarrow, artichokes, bittersweet berries, and catalpa pods.

The novice might find it helpful to trace the shape of the styrofoam on a large piece of paper first and lay on it the cones, nuts, berries, and other materials to be used for the garland. You can rearrange and alter until you have a composition that pleases you. You can easily repeat the pattern you have designed by removing one thing at a time and securing it to the styrofoam.

To fasten each cone, nut, or berry cluster to the garland, make a bed or "pocket" by pushing the end of it into the styrofoam. Remove the cone or whatever, add a blob of Elmer's glue, then force it back into the bed in the styrofoam. Since you want a symmetrical design, it is best to start in the center with your largest forms and work outward toward the tips. Be sure to have your material project slightly over the edges of the styrofoam.

Push Scotch pine into the styrofoam along the edges. No glue is needed as it is necessary to replace these fresh greens each year.

WHEAT AND ANGEL ON DOOR

In this decorative arrangement, the wheat was first tied together and fanned out to give a radiant effect behind

the angel. The angel, finished a natural pine color, matches very closely the golden color of the wheat, making for an interesting natural unity between the two. The bells are made of terra cotta painted in clear shades of yellow, blue, and orange; they hang from a wooden arch, with blue starflowers wired to the top of each bell.

The wheat sprays on the shutters are decorated with yellow strawflowers, blue starflowers, crabapples, and green grapes. Fine #30 wire is used to bind the flowers and grapes, but heavy #24 wire is needed for the apples. The ribbon-like material that encircles the fruits and flowers is a thin wooden hoop of natural wood.

The combination of the materials and colors gives this arrangement a Scandinavian feeling. Not only is this pleasant on a front door, but it would be very effective on a bare wall over a fireplace that has no mantelshelf.

CHAPTER TWO

ENTRANCE HALL DECORATIONS

HOUSE PLANT ARRANGEMENT

ONE OF my many groups of plants indoors is this one that greets you as you enter the front hall. The window reflected in the mirror faces west, so that a fair amount of sunlight streams across the hall to the plants. No blooming plants are kept here during the year except on special occasions like Christmas, when I add azaleas, poinsettias, cyclamen, or red-flowering kalanchoes. Any kind of ivy and any of the philodendrons, ficus, palms, and ferns grow successfully in this location. Angelwing begonia and beefsteak begonia also do well here.

The cherub is holding a styrofoam ball that has been covered with burdock burrs and sprayed copper to match the fountain bowls. Princess pine roping, draped as a garland, finishes the arch at the top of the mirror.

Growlux lights, concealed behind the arch, cast a soft glow every night and create a charming atmosphere. (The light also benefits the plants.)

CARVED ANGEL HEAD AND
DELLA ROBBIA WREATH

The angel head and Della Robbia wreath, shown on the *inside* of our front door, are hand-carved and finished in the natural pine wood color. A plaster or ceramic angel head could be used in place of the carved one. And you might use a wreath of real or artificial fruits (see page 136) in place of the carved wreath. The colors and textures of this whole composition give a very pleasing warm glow. It is perhaps a little different in color than most of our Christmas decorations, for the satin ribbon is two-tone, shading from clear yellow through the orange and red tints, and the satin baubles are in the same hues. Note that the small regular loops at the top left of the wreath which look like ribbon are the pods of the albizzia tree. This is a subtropical tree that grows as far north as Boston and flourishes south of Washington, D.C. The strap-shaped pods are chartreuse-colored when first purchased or gathered. By the next year they will have faded to a very soft brownish green.

The carved-wood wreath is backed with dried Southern magnolia leaves which have turned to a soft greenish brown. The backs of the magnolia leaves have an almost fur-like texture and are a light brown. (Don't hesitate to use the backs of leaves—many times they are more attractive than the front.) To make this wreath, first wrap a flat wire frame with brown cloth. Then simply staple on the magnolia leaves, overlapping them a little. How do you staple dry, brittle leaves without breaking them? The secret is to soak them overnight in warm water—they will become soft and pliable again.

TOPIARY TREE

This topiary tree is mounted on a pine board with a simple beveled edge, which can be painted any color you choose. (Mine is purple.)

Proportion is important in this design, so first decide on the size the panel should be. My panel is 8½ by 30 inches, the pot 4½ inches tall, the ¾-inch dowel 15 inches long, and the styrofoam ball 6 inches in diameter.

The tree stands in one half of a regular white plastic pot. To cut a pot in half, draw a line down the middle of one side, across the bottom, and up the other side as a saw guide. A fine-toothed hack saw is best to use. The cutting is sometimes an exasperating procedure due to the slipperiness of the pot, so have a little patience. Lay the pot on its side with the bottom pointing away from you and braced against a support low enough to permit your saw to pass over it. Saw each side separately, allowing the saw to contact the entire length of the pot while so doing. Then saw the bottom.

Attach the half pot to the board by making a small hole in the board on each side under the lip of the pot and as close to it as possible. Run a heavy wire under the lip and through the holes, twisting the ends tightly together in the back. Next fill the pot with styrofoam which has been cut to fit. Spread a little Elmer's glue over the top and cover with either sheet moss or peat moss.

Cut in half a styrofoam ball of the proper proportion. (This is easily done with a sharp knife.) Force a dowel into the center of the bottom of the styrofoam ball and also into the styrofoam in the pot. (You might wish to color the dowel first—mix a little oil paint, in a color such as burnt sienna, with turpentine and brush it on.)

Before putting greens on the styrofoam ball, cover it with sheet moss, which you attach with heavy wire hairpins. The reason for doing this is to cover any bare spots that might show between the greens. Then glue the ball and dowel to the board. Your styrofoam may slip and slide if you try to work on it too soon. If you use Elmer's glue, it will require some time to dry. Therefore, this is a good place to use a glue gun if you have one. The heated adhesive of a glue gun dries in a matter of seconds, which facilitates the assembly of the arrangement.

Sprigs of cedar, boxwood, or yew are the best choices for greens because they stand up well and are pleasant in texture. Taking pieces about 3 inches long, start at the middle of the top of the moss-covered styrofoam ball and insert them in a line down to the middle of the bottom. Next start at the center of one side and make a horizontal line to the center of the other side. There are now four triangular areas to be filled in. Don't hesitate to stud them well with your sprigs of greens.

If you wish to decorate your tree, kumquats, lady apples, crabapples, green grapes, or apricots are effective. All can be easily attached with toothpicks thrust into the styrofoam. You might finish the flower pot with bands of gold ribbon, glued at the base and top rim.

A pair of these topiary trees can be lovely, if you have a proper spot for them. Double doors (inside or out), a mantelpiece, any place where a balanced pair would look well are possibilities.

PAIR OF CONE DROPS

In some instances the most effective Christmas decorations are those that are in harmony with their surroundings yet are not too prominent. These two cone drops, for example, blend beautifully with the stenciled fiddleback bench below, yet do not overpower it.

These drops were made in the same manner as the drops explained on page 48. Painted clay bells were attached with wire to the bottoms of the ropes. The twining ribbon-like seed pods are from a catalpa tree. These are a reddish brown color on the outside and a golden buff on the inside, complementing the cut and whole spruce, hemlock, and pine cones.

The circles at the top of the drops were formed of acorns and small hemlock cones wired to pipe cleaners, the ends of which were connected to make a circle. (Little wreaths made this way may also be placed around candles or candlestick bases, by the way, but make sure not to set them too close where they might catch fire.)

BEACH STONE AND
PERIWINKLE WREATH

This wreath was created when our beach changed last summer from smooth sand to pebbles. There, with the help of three small granddaughters, we gathered the material for it. The green stones, perhaps because they were scarce, seemed to me to be the loveliest, and because they had to be of similar size, it took about a month to collect enough to make this 12-inch wreath.

Once in a while we would discover beautiful purple, pink, or yellow stones much too lovely to leave on the beach, so these were also collected. There were also occasional tiny yellow periwinkle shells. In sorting out the larger colored stones, I found I had enough purple ones to make two flowers, enough pink for two more flowers, and enough yellow for one flower. Each flower has five petals with a contrasting center. These five flowers do not show clearly in the black-and-white photograph, but if you look carefully, you will spot them, evenly spaced around the wreath.

Because the stones are quite heavy, a 12-inch circle of ⅜-inch plywood was made for a backing for the wreath. First we marked off the wreath into five even sections, then glued the stone flowers on with Elmer's glue

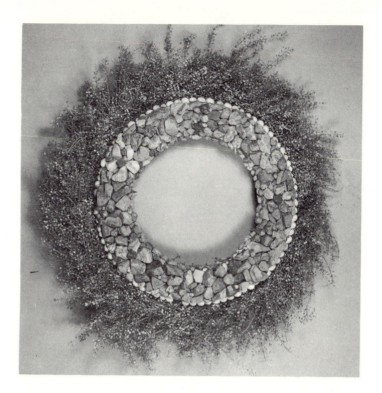

and filled in the entire wreath with the green stones except for the outer edge. We used the periwinkles for the outer edge and small stones to face the inner edge.

The process is similar to that of making any beach-pebble mosaic. Turn each stone about and try it at every angle until you find the closest fit for final placement.

The background wreath is pepper weed made in the manner described on pages 144 and 146.

ARCH WITH CONE DROP

In this decorative arrangement, the blue spruce used for the arch was wired to a shaped coat hanger (page 12). The two large Norway spruce cones at the top on either side were also secured to the coat hanger with #30-gauge wire, and held in place at both ends.

The string of cones hangs free and can be used in many different ways and sizes, according to the length of the rope you attach them to. First cut the rope a little longer than the desired finished length; tie two or three knots in the rope, about 5 inches apart. Assemble cones of different sizes, shapes, and colors. Cut some in flower forms and wire each cone separately lengthwise through the center. Fine #30 wire will do for the size of cones shown in the picture.

Starting at the bottom, wire some of the long tapering cones to the rope. Work from the bottom to the top, adding other kinds of whole and cut cones. When you have the swag about three-quarters finished, it is a good idea to hang it up on a wall or try it on the door. This will give you a chance to see how the cones hang and fall and where filling in with different sizes may be required. The first cones you wire on will be quite close to the roping, so that short lengths of wire may be used; but as you build up longer wires will be needed to enable you to fasten the cones between and around the other cones.

PRIMROSE WREATH

The background wreath is a 16-inch flat wire frame filled in with white pine. The inner wreath is made on a single

crinkle ring which was first wrapped with tape. You can make this wreath in the same manner as the dock wreath described on page 56.

The material used for this inner wreath is wild evening primrose, gathered and dried after it had gone to seed. Like dock, it is also a weed but has an entirely different color and texture. When dried it is a light sandy buff that, in some lights, has almost a golden glow. I have complemented this glow by using a gold bow at the bottom of the wreath. The carved angel at the top is of natural white pine, which blends well with the color of the evening primrose.

When wild primrose is picked but not used immediately, it may become brittle and dry, making it difficult to work with. Just soak it in warm water overnight and it will become soft again, pliable and easy to use.

STOCKING

If by chance you have or can obtain an old wooden stocking dryer, use it as a base for this stocking decoration. Otherwise, you can easily make one. Heavy cardboard is satisfactory if you plan to use the decoration inside your home. If it will be exposed to outside weather conditions, Masonite, pegboard, or plywood is more suitable and durable.

Most people find that drawing a leg with a foot properly attached is not easy. Use a little ingenuity. Have a friend with a shapely leg stand before a strong light, pointing her toe, so that the shadow of her leg and foot are cast upon the material to be used. Outline the sil-

houette with a soft pencil or crayon. If you are doing it on heavy cardboard, you can probably manage to cut this to shape. If you are using plywood or building board, a power jig saw, band saw, or saber saw will do the job in a hurry. Lacking these, you can do the job by hand with a keyhole saw. Ask your husband to saw it for you; if he is a "do-it-yourselfer," he will probably be glad to help.

After the leg has been cut, sandpaper the edges if the material is not cardboard. Pull a red or green stocking over it, or cover it with red or green cloth stretched and stapled to the back.

Next comes the gay and sparkling touch, made from a copper mesh pot scrubber called "Chore Girl." (These may be purchased in any five-and-ten-cent store or supermarket.) For kitchen use, it comes as a tightly wound ball, but by removing the pin or rivet that holds it together and then unwinding it, you will obtain a tube of attractive copper netting that is extremely rugged and will remain bright and sparkling in all kinds of weather. Pull the tube over the stocking, gather the toe and fold it over behind the foot and either pin, sew, or staple it to hold it securely. Leave the top of the stocking open so the decorations may be tucked in.

Use any kind of evergreen as a background for your baubles. For this particular stocking, I chose sprigs of cedar, green satin baubles tied together, and a bow of green satin copper-dotted ribbon to go on each side. The third bow was made from another Chore Girl (which also can double as an excellent copper ribbon).

To give an entirely different feeling to this decoration, use other materials to fill in the top of the stocking: children's toys, musical instruments, holly, California pepper berries, distinctively wrapped small packages of varying sizes, or what you will.

Hang the stocking by attaching a heavy wire to the back of the stocking frame.

CHAPTER THREE

LIVING ROOM
DECORATIONS

MADONNA PICTURE WITH ROPING
AND FRUIT ARRANGEMENT

ANY PICTURE or mirror may be used as a basis for this wall decoration. Choose an unframed picture with a Christmas motif which is somewhat smaller than the dimensions of the glass, and secure it to the glass of the picture or mirror with transparent tape. This does not disturb or injure the original picture in any way, and after Christmas it may easily be removed.

To make roping to frame the taped-on picture, use rope about as thick as a pencil and cut it long enough to go around the picture plus a little extra for good measure. Any of the finer evergreens serve here—cedar and boxwood are my favorites for this size of roping. Using #30 gauge, wire two or three pieces of greens in a bunch, then wire them to the rope. Each time overlap the pieces about one half their length. When the rope is covered, wire together the ends of the rope and tape it to the picture.

The arrangement below the picture is made in a wooden compote. First wire two small sprays of artificial grapes to the ends of two long sprays of cedar. Using a pin holder such as are used for flower arrangements, place the cedar sprays in the compote. Next add two pieces of Japanese andromeda and then the rather long sprays of

pepper berries. It is best to wire the pepper berries together at the base before you put them into the arrangement. A few lady apples complete the composition. To
hold them in place, add stems of the length desired. Willow branches are excellent for this use as willow bends so
nicely. Plunge one end of a willow branch into each apple
and insert the other end in the pin holder.

WREATH OF DOCK

This wreath is made from the seed heads of a lovely weed
called dock. Dock grows in spikes from 2 to 3 feet in
height and has a very delicate appearance but is most
rugged. Early in summer it is green tinged with rosy pink.
As the season progresses, it changes to light brown and
then to dark rust brown. It has thousands of little seed-
like parts and, as you are working with it, many will fall
off. In fact, your lap will be full of dock and the floor
will be covered with it, but there will still be plenty on
your wreath. I have a dock wreath that I have carried
about with me on my lectures for at least five years, and
it is still full and abundant.

For the base of this type of wreath use a single crinkle
ring. First wrap the ring with florist's tape to prevent the
wires you use to attach the dock from slipping. If florist's
tape is not available, you may use dark-colored cloth
strips. However, tape is quicker and neater.

The manner in which the material is applied to the
wreath makes this unusual design possible. Therefore,
first locate the middle of the top and the middle of the
bottom and wrap a piece of thin wire to mark each of
these places. Then apply the plant material. Work down

from the middle of the top to the middle of the bottom, first on one side and then the other.

Wire the dock to the ring in bunches of various sizes. Start at the top with only two or three single pieces. The size of the bunches should be increased as you progress to the middle of the bottom. Each bunch should overlap the preceding one.

Any number of different trimmings can be used to finish off the base. Just a simple gold ribbon bow is very effective with brown, soft red, or bright green ribbons. The trim I have used is a small string of pine and other cones, with two Southern magnolia leaves wired on each side behind them. I purposely displayed the backs of the magnolia leaves to show their rich brown color. The dock

wreath may be sprayed with gold or a color if you desire, but I prefer mine in its natural brown hues, with the various colors of the natural cones harmonizing with it.

Wheat, corn, pampas grass, and fern fronds are other variations that might be used for making this wreath. In place of the cones, you could use red crabapples, kumquats with euonymus berries, brass or plastic bells, glass baubles, satin or velvet baubles.

DOCK WREATH WITH CANDELABRUM

Some people might consider a wreath made of weeds too informal to use with a crystal candelabrum. However, I feel that a somewhat formal wreath made of dock is lacy and delicate enough to complement this candelabrum. I removed the center candle and replaced it with princess pine sprays and a cluster of gold baubles tied with a gold ribbon.

To give color balance and also to add visual weight, I placed small brown hemlock cone wreaths around the two remaining candles. Directions for making the small wreaths are given in detail on pages 140-41. However, if the arrangement was left this way, it still would not be balanced. The base of the candelabrum is too small to equal the visual weight created by the small cone wreaths.

To solve this problem, I have made two flat wreaths and placed them around the base of the candelabrum. The 16-inch ring I covered with punchinello, which is the gold material left after sequins have been punched from it. It is available at better florist's shops. Then I wrapped a 14-inch ring with plain gold ribbon and set it inside the punchinello ring. The simple placement of these two rings gives balance and ties the whole composition together.

POINSETTIA ARRANGEMENT

This arrangement is an effective way to use cut poinsettias, which during the Christmas season are readily available from the florist. But in this particular arrangement, better-than-average artificial poinsettias can be tastefully combined with freshly cut flowers and plant material. Most artificial flowers, including the poinsettias sold by most department stores, are not worth carrying home, but truly lifelike poinsettias can occasionally be found at a fair price. With a little care they can be used for many years.

For the container, I used an old metal lamp base from which the socket and wiring had been removed. (This is one of my treasures found in a junk shop.) The opening was enlarged to permit a large cup pinholder to be inserted. Its pleasing classical design, its coloring of tones of pale green and ivory and dull gold fluting give this container an elegance that supplements, accents, and blends with practically any combination of flowers and foliage. However, a painted wood, alabaster, china, or pottery urn would also be very suitable.

The finished design here consists of sprays of Japanese yew cut from the garden, dried wild asters, real white poinsettia blossoms, cream-colored carnations, and Rex begonia leaves from a house plant. As suggested above, artificial poinsettias may be used, but these blossoms were cut from potted plants. Actually they are not pure white, but a soft creamy color with a tinge of green. They blend beautifully with the light ivory-and-green color of the container.

The background consists of two arching branches of yew, one of my favorite background materials; it is ex-

ceptionally long lasting, usually holds its freshness for weeks when kept in water. Large sprays of euonymus, boxwood, or cedar could be used in place of the yew.

Against this rich background, I placed bunches of buff-colored dried wild asters. If you wire the slender stems together in bunches of varying sizes (using #30-gauge wire), you can insert the sprays as a unit in the pin holder. It is much easier to work with them in this fashion than by using single stems.

These little asters, by the way, are the kind that grow wild alongside roads and in fields. We gather them in September and dry them. We place them in a container with a normal amount of water, and leave them until the water has evaporated. This way they dry slowly, retaining their color and form much better than by other methods of quick drying.

Next, I added four cream-colored carnations for variety of form and texture, and finally I put in a few suitable-sized leaves from a Rex begonia. Soft green in color, edged by and backed with rich mahogany, they give life to the whole arrangement and add a final touch of elegance. The size of these leaves furnishes not only the mass but also the weight and balance needed to complete the picture.

In winter, large leaves of colored foliage are scarce, but house plants can be a prime source of this material. The begonia family is exceptional in this respect. By using begonia leaves in decorative arrangements, you get two results: while they are in the arrangement, they are also making roots so that later on, the leaves can be potted to make new plants. Leaves of Rex begonias in prime condition are more likely to produce roots if a small portion of the rootstalk or main stem is taken with the leaf.

GOLD LAMÉ WREATH AND CANDELABRUM

One of the interesting dividends of being a lecturer is the odd things people give you. A lady gave me an old gold lamé dress. She was "sure she would never wear it again and anyhow it had a hole in it." I was more than

delighted with the gift. The color and texture pleased me, and the hole was no trouble at all—I just cut around it to make 4-inch strips.

I wrapped a 16-inch flat wire ring with the lamé strips, turning in ½ inch on one edge as I wrapped. One-inch gold fringe sewed to the outside edge gave it a nice finish.

Hanging inside the lamé wreath is a small wreath in green, brown, and pink colors. I made this on a 10-inch styrofoam circle, covering it first with sheet moss. This can be either glued on or secured with heavy wire hairpins or heavy wire bent into hairpin shapes. I wired small bunches of pink starflowers together with fine wire, then attached them to the wreath with heavy wire hairpins. The open shells of the copper beechnut have stems strong enough to thrust into the styrofoam; it is more effective to use three or four close together. The small brown hemlock cones glued to the styrofoam complete this wreath. The soft gray-green of the sheet moss, combined with the rich brown of the cones, the buff color of the copper beechnut burrs, and the delicate pink flowers, gives an old-world look to this wreath.

The girandole is decorated with small sprays of princess pine and pink starflowers, which were tucked into the irregularities of the metalwork around the candles. The candles are soft beige-pink, almost the color of the walls. The painted hand-carved angel echoes quiet pinks and gold.

BASKET WITH MUSICAL INSTRUMENTS

Although this may look complicated, it really is not at all difficult to make.

Start with a green garden stake, either wood or bamboo. This may sound odd, but it is the backbone of the design which holds everything together. The stake should be long enough to include the bow, basket, and fruit. Get a basket and spray it with gold.

For a bow with a sculptured look, use soft gray-green velvet ribbon with stiffening in it. This is a special kind of ribbon and may be purchased at better florist's or garden shops. Attach the bow to the top of the stake with fine #30 wire and let the streamers fall freely to below the end of the stake. Wire the basket to the stake, fastening the top of it as well as the bottom, and then fill it with styrofoam. Directly under the basket, wire to the stake a piece of styrofoam about 3 by 5 inches. Now the preliminaries are over and the fun begins.

Many different materials and color combinations can make up this arrangement. First assemble the fruits, flowers, seed pods, berries, leaves, etc. you intend to use. In my basket are large dried woods roses, clusters of small woods roses, wild cucumber pods, dried hydrangeas, dried oak leaves, dried croton leaves, Japanese andromeda, sprigs of fresh Hinoki cypress, and catalpa seed pods. If their stems were long and strong enough, they were simply thrust into the styrofoam. Stems that were not were wired to toothpicks, which were pushed into the styrofoam. The two musical instruments from a toy shop were sprayed with gold, then wired to the bottom of the piece of styrofoam under the basket.

The grapes, the only artificial fruits, were attached to the styrofoam with heavy wire hairpins. All the other fruits are real, either fresh or dried. I use no special method for drying fruits. I find that many of them simply dry slowly while they are part of an arrangement, retaining their form and some of their natural color.

Lemons and limes in several sizes which had become very lightweight when dry were used here; they were easily glued to the styrofoam. Fresh Hinoki cypress and oak leaves, dried hydrangeas, and wild cucumbers were tucked between the fruits.

The color scheme of this arrangement includes the soft gray-green of the ribbon; the gold of the basket, musical instruments, and the candlesticks; the blue-purple of the artificial grapes. (Bunches of the grapes are also wired on the candlesticks.) The other fruits are soft greens and pale yellows; the hydrangeas, light blue to purple; and the woods roses are creamy inside, rich brown on the outside.

It is very easy to make substitutions in the contents of the basket if you wish, as well as to change the kinds of leaves and evergreens.

MUSSEL SHELL WREATH

On the beach one January day, while picking up seaweed, I discovered an abundance of mussel shells that had been washed up. (We always go to the beach in January after a storm to gather seaweed because it is full of minerals and very good for the garden.) The shells were so beautiful, I brought home a basketful, and they stayed all winter in the shed along with my collection of pine and other cones.

Summer is a wonderful time of year to make Christmas decorations for you are less pressed for time than in December. I make all of my permanent decorations in summer. One warm August day I decided to do something with the mussels. As I picked each shell out of the

basket, I ran my thumb over the inside to wipe out anything that might have collected there during the winter.
I discovered that it was not necessary to wash them at all
—having been exposed to the weather, they were clean
of sand and had no sea or shellfish odor. My thumb gave
them a splendid polish. If you have never looked inside a
mussel shell, you would be surprised to find it has a
texture very similar to that of porcelain.

The outsides have a very flat, deep blue-and-black coloring, while the insides are shaded from deep blue at the
tips through varying shades of light blue to white.

I had various sizes of shells. Some were fully opened
with the two inner sides separated; some were partly
opened with the two sides still connected. I first sorted
them for size and form. As I arranged the shells in many
different ways, butterflies, pond lilies, and all sorts of interesting compositions took shape. Finally I chose the
one shown in the picture in which five shells were used
for each flower. All the shells in the large wreath had
both halves connected. The pair of shells placed toward
the outside edge of the wreath were the largest and most
fully open; the other three pairs were about half open.
This allows lovely light-and-shadow play and gives a
wonderful contrast between the flat, dark finish on the
outer surfaces of the shells and the beautiful porcelain-
like finish on the inner surfaces.

A circle of plywood or Masonite makes a suitable background on which to make this wreath. When using any
wood surfaces as a background for gluing purposes, by
the way, leave the wood in its natural state so that its
pores are open to receive the glue. This will afford the
strongest bond between the wood and the material being
glued to it.

After the shells had set and were securely in place, I

applied the glue to the wreath between the shells, to hold the moss. (If the spaces are too small to allow your fingers to get between, use a knitting needle, orange-wood stick, or something similar to pack the moss in place.) I then glued small yellow periwinkle shells to the centers from which the mussel shells radiated simulating flower centers.

I made the small wreaths on circles of heavy cardboard. Five large, fully opened separate shells and five pairs of smaller shells were used, with sheet moss packed between. Then, to the backs of these wreaths I stapled loops of ribbon in a color that almost exactly matched the sheet moss.

I display my shell wreath on a 16-inch wire frame which has been wrapped and filled in with gold lamé (see page 64). When filling in the center of any wreath, I find it easier to pin in the background instead of sewing. This allows you to remove the background quickly and easily when you want a change.

It is curious the way the color of the sheet moss and gold lamé blend together. A study in textures and combinations of odd materials, they form a most effective decoration.

PINK MADONNA WITH WREATH

Because the walls and mantel in this room are a soft brownish pink, we used here a large background wreath of buff-colored pepper weed (see pages 144 and 146. The leafy antique-gold clock frame was hung next, and on top of that we placed a small peach, prune, and cherry stone wreath that had been sprayed with gold (for details on

making it, see pages 142-43). Each wreath hangs by a separate wire, and all wires are wound together by a length of gold fringe. A bow of gold ribbon at the top hides the hanger.

The hand-carved Madonna in a soft pink robe stands on a pewter-washed copper container turned upside down.

The matching side arrangements are displayed on stands of three separate parts each. The flowers and berries are set in pin holders placed in small alabaster urns.

These urns are set on top of hand-carved wooden candle-sticks which have been inverted. The carved fruits at the top and bottom of the candlesticks are painted in natural fruit colors; the rest is antique gold.

The fluted wooden bases are painted gray and gold to match the Madonna's pewter-washed copper base. As a substitute for these bases, try brass, pewter, or silver bowls; odd pieces of marble, old fluted electric light fix-tures, tin trays, large ash trays; try almost anything until you find objects that are in proper balance with the whole composition.

The flowers used in the side arrangements are small wild white asters which, when dried, turn cream color. Wrap four or five of the small stems together with fine wire and put bunches of them in the center of each pin holder. Fill in around the bottom with pink pepper ber-ries and mauve-colored starflowers, also wired in bunches before insertion in the pin holder. These arrangements are extremely simple, but the soft textures of the material used, the blending of the flower and berry colors with the painted fruit, plus the height attained by the three-part pedestals give the whole design a good deal of distinction.

ANGEL AND IVY TREES

The frames for these ivy trees were made from wire coat hangers, which are heavy enough to stand stiffly and support the ivy, but are also pliant enough to bend and work easily.

For each pot of ivy, use three coat hangers to build a kind of cage. Cut the hook off each hanger and straighten

Wire frame made of coat hangers

out the long wire. Bend the three pieces of wire into the shape you wish for the tree and bind them together at the top with electrician's plastic tape. At about the middle of the wires, use a fourth coat hanger wire horizontally to space the perpendicular ones. Bend the horizontal piece around each perpendicular piece to keep them the proper distance apart. Push the three lower ends into the earth in a pot of ivy. The cage is now ready for the ivy to be trained upon it and wired lightly in place.

The ribbon-like bows on these ivy trees are made from the chartreuse-colored seed pods of the albizzia tree, described on page 41.

Pink ceramic pots hold the ivy trees. Inverted alabaster containers serve as bases to give the visual weight needed to balance the height of the trees.

The wreaths under the mantel are small circles of styrofoam with maple tree seed pods glued on. Wide chartreuse satin ribbons fall gracefully from these, the bows protruding through the wreaths.

MADONNA AND WHITE PINE WREATHS

These white pine wreaths above the mantel were made on 12-inch flat wire frames so as to encircle a special pair of gold frames. When this picture was taken, the pine wreaths were two years old. Because they had not dropped their needles when taken down after the first season, they were carefully put away for use the next year. New life was given to them then, by a spraying of gold paint. Besides changing the color, spraying also helps to hold the needles fast, and wreaths thus treated will last for many years.

Within the wreaths and gold frames are small but deep metal pie plates from the five-and-ten-cent store, sprayed gold. A Christmas card picture was cut to fit and glued to the bottom of each plate. Fine #30 wire is strong enough to hold these little plates; it was taped to each back with a loop to hang by. Since the pie plates are just a bit smaller than the fancy gold frames, a circle of wall color shows between the two. A lovely dark shadow is cast by the deep sides of the pie plates. Although these are simple and fun to make, they also are very effective.

The statue is the Madonna of the World, with Jesus as a small boy standing on the globe, obtainable from religious supply stores. Its colors are off-white, gold, and blue. Assorted cones cut in various forms have been wired together and placed at the feet; on each side is a bunch of dried pink hydrangea flowers backed with gilded magnolia leaves. The garland under the mantel is described on page 77.

HOLY FAMILY, HOLLY WREATH, AND GARLAND

One nice thing about holly leaves is that they curl so beautifully when they dry out. We made a wreath of dried holly leaves on a styrofoam base. The holly stem is strong enough to stick into styrofoam, which is what we did. You stick the stem in, pull it out, and fill the hole with a few drops of Elmer's glue. Then force the holly-leaf stem into the hole, manipulating it so that it will curl around and overlap other leaves on the face of the

wreath. The inside and outside edges of the wreath do not show in this picture, but to finish these edges, we chose copper beechnut burrs, securing them to the wreath by the same procedure as for the holly leaves. When the wreath was completed, we sprayed the holly leaves and beechnut burrs with gold paint, and wired a little cluster of princess pine to the top of the wreath.

A few gilded holly leaves with especially nice curves were chosen to be inserted among the sprigs of princess pine on the mantel.

The old candelabrum behind the Holy Family statue is trimmed with gold fringe. A single angel or Madonna might be used in place of the Holy Family.

Garland or Swag

The base of this decoration was a piece of plywood cut to shape (see page 14). All material was secured to it with Elmer's glue.

Because this is a symmetrical design, it would be best to sort out your materials before starting to glue. Make sure you have plenty of flowers, berries, seed pods, cones, and whatever else you choose, to assure that both sides will be alike. Start at the bottom tip of one side drop and work upwards to the corner; Complete one side and then repeat the procedure for the other.

The materials used here were: seven large dried woods roses (two at the top of each drop, and three at the center of the garland), various sizes and kinds of cones, seed pods of poppy, teasel, dock, Japanese andromeda. Carefully dried flowers of celosia, hydrangea, tansy, and Queen Anne's lace are used for grace notes. The cone in the middle, cut lengthwise, is a Norway spruce.

To make the swag full and abundant be sure to use plenty of material. Don't forget to cover all edges, as well as the surface. Flowers and small berries can be tucked between and placed on top of the larger materials.

ANGEL WITH BOXWOOD TREES
AND WREATHS

These two boxwood wreaths were made in the same way as the dock wreath described on page 56.

The way these double wreaths are hung is what makes them unusual. First, wire both wreaths together at the bottom. Hang the back wreath flat against the wall, allowing the front wreath to project out above the angel's head. String a fine wire of the proper length from the top of the back wreath to the top of the front wreath, to hold the front wreath at the angle you wish.

The trees are made of styrofoam cones covered with

small boxwood sprays. Start at the top with small short pieces, increasing the length and bushiness of the branches as you work down toward the bottom of the cone. Wire stars of gold tinsel atop the trees.

Here, trees are set in footed alabaster urns placed on upside down ceramic pots of a soft pink that matches the angel's dress. These pedestals add the visual weight needed to balance that of the trees.

The small bells at the top of the wreaths are pink and gold, matching the angel's horn and the stars on the trees.

ARTICHOKE, GRAPE, AND
PINEAPPLE MANTEL GARLAND

This elegant but simple mantel garland combines fresh fruits with the greenery of a wreath and roping. First make a 16-inch princess pine wreath (see page 6 for

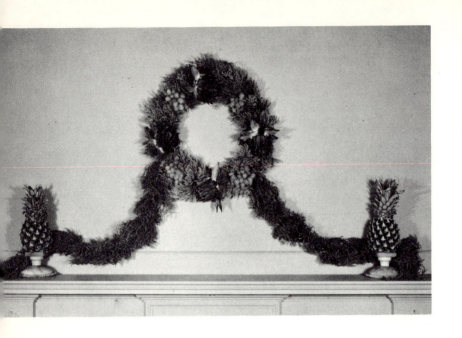

details). Decorate the wreath with four similar-size bunches of grapes and four artichokes placed alternately. Use fine wire to attach the grapes.

Paraffin, by the way, seems to keep the outer petals of the artichokes open quite well. Hold the petals open carefully for they bruise easily and will turn brown if injured (actually you need three hands for this operation). While the petals are held open, pour warm paraffin in the crevices between the petals. The paraffin hardens quickly and prevents the petals from closing. Heavy wire forced through the butt end of the artichoke can be used to secure it to the wreath.

Princess pine roping flows in a graceful line from the wreath to encircle the fresh pineapples set on top of inverted alabaster urns.

CHAPTER FOUR

DINING ROOM DECORATIONS

CANDLE, HOLLY WREATH, AND BELLS

A TABLE decoration that is quite simple, easy to create, and very practical has three permanent units that can be used in a number of different ways: the flat wreath, the bells, and the holly wreath.

First, wrap a 16-inch flat wire frame with wide red satin ribbon, to make a wreath that can be saved from year to year. It is wonderfully helpful to have something ready to use as a base for next Christmas.

The ring of bells is the next unit. They are available on Christmas ornament counters, often in five-and-ten-cent stores. They come in different sizes, in blue, green, gold, and red, or they may come in mixed colors. They have a clear, bright, shiny finish and are unbreakable. Wrap a 16-inch crinkly wire frame with florist's tape and using fine #30 wire, attach each bell to this wreath ring, or tie each bell on with a bow of narrow red ribbon, being sure to tie a double knot. The bells should be spaced far enough apart so that each one sits flat. Place this wreath of bells on top of the red ribbon wreath.

To make the holly wreath, wrap a 12-inch crinkly wire frame with florist's tape. Using fine #30 wire, secure to it sprays of artificial holly. Wrap a 12-inch flat wire frame with red satin ribbon and wire the holly wreath to its outer rim. This versatile decoration can be displayed in many different ways. In this design, it was placed atop the wreath of bells, with small sprays of real cedar tucked between the holly leaves.

The large green sculptured candle in the center echoes the dark green linen of the tablecloth.

For an unusual place card holder, put a spool of red silk thread with a birthday candle in the top on one of the bells, and tie on a sprig of holly with narrow red satin ribbon.

In planning a table setting, it is wise to keep in mind everything that will be on the table. There will, of course, be the decorations, possibly candles, the china and glassware—to say nothing of the food itself. This creates quite a bit of design and color. Confusion being the element we should try to avoid in all designs, it has always seemed to me best to use plain colored or white cloths for a dining room table. This provides an uncluttered background that enhances and unifies the elements.

CANDELABRUM WITH PEPPER BERRIES

This silver candelabrum is one of my favorite centerpieces for my dining room table. The glass epergnes, which can be removed, make it possible to use it in many different ways. It is convenient to be able to consolidate the arrangement and candles in one container especially if the table is not large. The branch epergnes in this instance are filled with small bunches of princess pine and pepper berries. The center one has been removed. Care must be exercised when candle burning to avoid setting fire to the greens.

A silver cake plate was inverted to create a base, giving added height and importance, and filling in the space between the candelabrum and the inner wreath. This wreath, made on a 12-inch flat wire frame, was wrapped with salmon-colored velvet, a color that matches the color of the chair seats and ties in with the pink pepper berries in the arrangement.

Princess pine roping is the basic material of the outer wreath, with bunches of pepper berries wired on—the same combination as in the epergnes. The white candles match the Parian ware cherubs holding horns of plenty, which have been filled with sprigs of princess pine and pink starflowers.

CANDELABRUM AND GLASS GRAPES

Another arrangement using my silver candelabrum employs materials that are entirely artificial. The glass baubles make it very gay and sparkly. You could follow the same basic design and, by substituting real fruits, berries, and greens, create a completely different effect. Grapes, crabapples, cranberries, or any other small fruits would be suitable. Real white pine roping would be excellent in place of the artificial roping shown.

The candelabrum stands in a large silver pie server that is encircled inside and outside with artificial green roping from the five-and-ten-cent store. Bunches of silver bauble grapes (also from the five-and-ten-cent store) were placed at the sides to break up the circle and make a more interesting design—and one more suited to an oblong table. Green velvet leaves were tucked in between the grapes.

When you are buying glass baubles, select the kind with stems instead of rings on the ends for they are much easier to work with. You can make different-sized wreaths by winding the stems together at intervals and shaping them into a circle. This is what has been done at the base of the candelabrum and also around candle bases. The baubles in the center epergne are graduated in size and shaded in color from dark green upward to yellow-green that ties in with the yellow-green candles.

CANDELABRUM WITH FRUIT

This is not really a candelabrum at all—it is an old brass chandelier turned upside down. I discovered it in a secondhand store and immediately bought it for its lovely shape. The sockets that had held light bulbs now hold the candles. The brass cups on which prisms had been hung, now turned upside down, make perfect holders for fruits, flowers, berries, and other materials. Here I have placed green grapes in two of them, crabapples in the other two, with bits of yew tucked between and around the fruit.

The base of the chandelier is encircled with a wide, braided, gold choker necklace. It just exactly fits and gives weight and interest to the bottom. Save all your old costume jewelry—you can never tell when you might have just the right piece to add a bit of distinction to one of your creations.

The wreath outside the base is styrofoam decorated with brown satin ribbon, gold ribbon, and gold paper braid used in découpage work. The brown ribbon is glued to the outer rim and is edged with the gold braid both top and bottom. The pleated gold ribbon on the face of the wreath is secured with heavy wire shaped into hairpins. Make a pleat and force the wire through the ribbon and into the styrofoam. This will hold the ribbon down in the middle, yet allow it to stand up a bit along the edges. The wire hairpins disappear in the gold ribbon when they are firmly pushed through the ribbon into the styrofoam.

PINEAPPLE AND DELLA ROBBIA WREATH

A 16-inch flat wire frame wrapped with dull gold ribbon makes a rich background for a Della Robbia wreath composed of fresh fruit—green grapes, green crabapples, and small yellow crabapples; dried apricots; dried blue starflowers and yellow strawflowers; and andromeda leaves. The basic wreath is a 12-inch flat wire frame that has been wrapped with cloth then filled in with yew. A detailed explanation of how this wreath is assembled can be found on pages 136-39.

Around the candlesticks are small wreaths of yew and green crabapples. They can either be made on small crinkly wire frames, or on roping shaped into rings. The green crabapples are wired on in both cases.

The yellow and tawny colorings of the partly ripe pineapple are picked up and echoed by the apricots, yellow crabapples, and yellow flowers in the wreath. The pineapple is raised slightly by a gray metal base. The candlesticks are of gray and gold metal.

IRON CONTAINERS WITH CANDLES AND PINEAPPLES

This decorative group could be used in any number of different rooms. It would be interesting on a front hall table, on a mantel, or on a console table, and because it looks equally well from all sides, it could be used on a dining room table. The center container is a Franklin

stove top. It has a rather dramatic feeling as the containers are black iron antiqued with greenish-blue paint to give them a bronzy color. On the Franklin stove top I have placed a circle of wood that has six holes of suitable size bored in it to hold candles. Candle boards may be made in many shapes for use in other ways. They are usually long blocks of wood about 2 inches wide and of various lengths to hold from two to a dozen or more candles.

The side containers are a rather odd combination of things. For the tops, two flag stands, and for the bases, two old kerosene lamps. These are more interesting when accented with velvet ribbon or cloth laced through the eyelets. I have woven a dull yellow-green material through mine to enhance the unripened pineapples. The candles are also yellow-green. The evergreen is Scotch pine.

Real Franklin stove tops are a bit hard to find today. However, good reproductions are available in better florist shops. Look for unusual comparable pieces in antique shops, junk or secondhand shops, or in any good hunting ground.

DRIED FRUIT WREATH

To some people, dried fruits and flowers are not at all appealing—they are merely dead. To me, fruits take on an attractive, mellow patina in drying that cannot be attained in any other way.

It may take quite a long time to collect and dry enough fruits for a wreath like this, but the result is worth the waiting. When you finally have a good number, sort them out to make sure you will have enough

for even balance in the design. Lay them on a styrofoam wreath frame, trying them in a number of different patterns. Some fruits may be cut if they are too bulky to be used whole. In the wreath shown here, the pineapple, pomegranates, artichoke, and lemon were all cut in half. All but the pineapple can be easily cut with a saw-tooth-edged kitchen knife. Cut straight down through the pomegranate starting just to one side of the blossom end. Both sections are usable. Starting at the bottom of the pineapple, cutting is easy until you reach the top or crown. Then a saw is needed, as the top is extremely hard.

When cut, most fruits will have only a thin edge of rind left to use for gluing purposes. This makes it necessary to wire the fruits in place temporarily until the glue has hardened. Use the same method in making this fruit wreath as that given for the pine cone Heritage wreath on pages 139-41.

Dried fruits in this wreath: one pineapple, two pomegranates, one lemon, one artichoke—all cut and both halves used; whole lemons, limes, crabapples, quince, tangerines; avocado seeds, seeds from Japanese lanterns; apricots and raisins. The raisins and apricots were glued on last to fill in the interstices between the larger fruits. I covered the inside and outside edges of the wreath with petals cut from the artichokes, each glued on to overlap the next by about one-third. It is not practical to wire them on temporarily, but large common pins, placed one at each end, will hold the petals in place until the glue has set. Next day you can remove the pins by twisting them back and forth four or five times before pulling them out—this frees the pins from the glue, preventing them from pulling off the petals, too.

In making a wreath such as this, an electric glue gun, see page 18, is excellent because the hot adhesive dries very quickly (a matter of seconds) and there is no need for wires to hold the fruit in place.

I use no special technique for drying fruits and vegetables but merely let them dry in arrangements in an uncovered container at normal room temperature. On one end of a long bench in our family room, I always have a fruit and/or vegetable arrangement that varies with the time of year. In January, for example, the large basic fruits and vegetables in the container have remained since late September. There are two yellow crookneck squashes, four large and two small Eat-All squashes. The latter were dark green with light green stripes when first picked and put into the arrangement. Their colors have now changed to a soft light green with orange stripes. Five artichokes complete the basic design. As the season progresses, a variety of smaller fruits, flowers, seed pods, berries, and greens are used to vary the character of this arrangement. Red crabapples and kumquats are added for the Christmas season, with yew and holly tucked in here and there for a note of greenery.

Artichokes turn brown as they dry; they are the quickest and easiest of all vegetables or fruits to dry as they very seldom rot or mildew. Summer squashes dry to a deep orange and are a little shriveled at the neck. Eat-All squashes will dry quite firm. Crabapples and the kumquats will have a rough wrinkled surface when dry. All fruits and vegetables will shrink while drying, some more than others. For instance, a pineapple when fully dry will be only half its original size. It is difficult to tell exactly how long it will take to complete the drying of any particular fruit, for much will depend on its initial condition. Some may take almost a year.

First the fruit will start to soften and the skin becomes wrinkled. Some fruits such as pineapples will become extremely soft, almost mushy, and you may be tempted to throw them out. Soon, however, the outside skin should harden as the inside pulp dries. Occasionally it does not harden and the fruit has to be discarded. (At this stage in the drying process you may have to use a bug bomb spray to control the fruit flies.) The textures and contours of the fruit change as the drying progresses—lemons, for instance, often become grooved, while apples become rough all over. Pineapples will form mildew, but this can be brushed off later when they are completely dry, or it may be washed out with a small paint brush dipped in turpentine.

Many other fruits, berries, and seed pods could be dried and substituted for those in my wreath. Also, if you wish a bit more color on the fruit, brush on a small amount of pigment dissolved in a little turpentine. For instance, a little burnt sienna (a brown oil paint) diluted in turpentine and brushed on a pineapple enhances the natural effect, and is especially good to use where the mildew has been. Apply any paint in only the thinnest of coatings to give tints that soak immediately into the fruit, creating a natural color effect.

CHAPTER FIVE

BEDROOM
DECORATIONS

BEDROOM WREATH

THIS IS an extremely delicate wreath that can be hung in a young girl's room or any feminine bedroom—or even in a powder room—to give holiday color. It has graced my bedroom door, and the colors were chosen to blend with the bedroom decor—delicate pink, white, and soft, grayed yellow-green. The basic part of this wreath may be wrapped with any color you choose to convey whatever feeling you want.

First wrap a 12-inch flat wire frame with tarlatan, a sheer, stiff material used for ballet skirts, cut in straight strips about 1½ inches wide. Three yards of strips are needed to wrap a 12-inch ring, 5 yards for a 16-inch one. A few colors are available in department stores, but theatrical supply shops carry a great range of colors. You may want to make several wreaths because the colors are so luscious. Nylon net could be used instead of tarlatan and is readily available wherever yard goods are sold.

Wrap the ring firmly, for this is the base to which you will sew gathered, fluffy material. Cut more strips of tarlatan 14 inches wide, fold in half once, then in half again, making four layers 3½ inches wide. Cut on the folds. Using a large needle and matching thread, sew through the middle of all four layers of the material. The stitches need not be fine—a running or basting stitch will do, or it can be done on a sewing machine. Then pull one of the threads to gather the tarlatan. (If you have a gathering attachment on your machine, that is what you would use here.) Next sew the gathered strip around the middle of the wrapped wreath. Continue making these gathered strips and sewing them to the wreath wrapping until the circle is completed. To create the fluffiness, separate the four layers by firmly pulling apart each layer. As the four layers are separated and pulled apart, they stand out stiffly and firmly, resembling a tutu.

Even if nothing further were done on the wreath, it would be beautiful. I often use mine just this way. However, the one shown here was loosely wrapped with Hamburg edging and soft green ribbon. Bunches of pink starflowers with rosettes of green ribbon were sewed on at intervals.

The center flower wreath was made on a crinkle ring using various-size bunches of pink starflowers in the same manner as the dock wreath detailed on page 56.

A wide pink satin bow at the bottom puts the final touch to the double wreath. Whatever color scheme you choose or whatever materials you use, a gay, fluffy, feminine wreath is always a joy.

This same type of wreath can be used in other parts of the house in different colors and with different kinds of trim. For instance, for a living room, the net or tarlatan could be dark green and yellow and orange artificial fruits could replace the starflowers. In the kitchen, a wreath of red with small white onions would be appropriate. For the bathroom, a monochromatic one in shades of blue, with satin baubles and velvet bows, might be interesting.

BEDROOM WALL DECORATION AND TREE

This wall group in my bedroom is not all put away after Christmas. The cherub was a gift that means more than just Christmas, and the wreath is not so Christmasy that it cannot remain all year.

I made the wreath on a circle of heavy cardboard, which was kept firm and rigid by a wrapping of a closely woven piece of cloth. If wreaths this size are merely to be used for a color background, they may be wrapped with ribbon, but if they are to be decorated, more support is needed—hence, the firm material.

I wound small bunches of pink starflowers with fine wire and wired them to the wreath, overlapping each bunch enough to cover the stems. Then I inserted four bunches of lavender starflowers at even intervals around the wreath.

The two porcelain cherubs playing musical instruments were designed to hold candles, but I fitted them with flowers instead—one or two small pieces of princess pine, tiny bunches of pink and lavender starflowers, artificial violets, tiny artificial pink rosebuds, and dried real pink geraniums. The Italian wall shelf is painted soft green.

The tree on top of the desk was made on a styrofoam cone. First I wrapped it with white artificial roping from the five-and-ten-cent store. (Real evergreen roping could be substituted, of course.) Anchor the roping at the bottom with a heavy wire hairpin. Spiral to the top of the cone and anchor again. Then I wound a band of 1-inch pink velvet ribbon from the bottom to the top of the tree, leaving the white roping showing between. The small pale pink rosebuds, which match those in the wreath above, have firm stems, so I could insert them in the styrofoam at regular intervals.

The tree stands on a Chinese gilded teakwood base. Around the base are trimmings from a spring hat, used just as they came off the hat—nothing added. (Be sure to look carefully at your hats before discarding them—some of the best artificial flowers are millinery ones, and they are sometimes hard to get.) This spray happened to be pink and white flowers and buds with green velvet leaves, but any other colors might be used. Or you might use real or artificial greens, with flowers placed here and there.

DECORATIONS FOR A MAN'S BEDROOM OR DEN, A YOUNG BOY'S BEDROOM AND A YOUNG GIRL'S BEDROOM

The decoration at the center bottom of the photograph is just right for a man's bedroom. To make this, dried fern fronds were tied together and then fanned out. This forms a background against which a five-and-ten-cent store violin was displayed—in this case, indicative of one of my husband's hobbies. Against such a background any other item of significance could be equally well displayed as long as it was of a proper size.

Another design suitable for a man's or a boy's bedroom would be the star. The star is cut from a piece of inch-thick pine with a saw. It is then given one coat of orange shellac. Of course, you could paint or spray it any color if you preferred. Use the electric glue gun (see page 18) to glue the pine cones to the star board. Because the glue from the gun sets almost instantly, make sure each cone is properly placed.

The top center wreath is masculine enough to suit young boys. This consists of three parts, first a 16″ flat wire frame was wrapped with cloth and then cedar and white pine were tucked in. Directions for making this are on page 5. The second part is a 12-inch flat wire frame wrapped with strips of green burlap. The third part

is braided raffia which was wound loosely around the green burlap wreath. Hemp or other types of rope could be used.

The pine cone angel, ideal for a young girl's bedroom, is simple and very easy to make with the use of a glue gun. The body is made from two cones from a white pine tree. The head is a dried lemon. The hat is a dried artichoke. The hair is dried princess pine, the eyes are cloves, the mouth is a small seed of the copper beech, the wings and skirt dried magnolia leaves, and the collar and cuffs petals of dried artichoke. The two pine cones which form the body should be the same size. With the scales of one facing up and those of the other facing down, force them together so as to interlock them, then glue. The pine-cone arms and legs are wired to the body using fine wire. This holds them in place so that they can be glued.

To attach the head, the scales on the stem end of the pine cone were trimmed to make a point which was then inserted in a hole in the neck end of the lemon. A large amount of glue was used to make a bond between the two. Then the princess pine was glued to the top of the lemon for hair. To make the hat remove the center of a dried artichoke, turn it upside down and simply glue it on. Single artichoke leaves were glued around the neck and cuffs. Magnolia leaves were glued on for wings and skirt.

STARFLOWER WREATH WITH ANGEL

This is a very feminine wreath which would delight a young girl. It consists of two wreaths. The outer one is

a 16-inch flat wire frame on which pink satin ribbon has been wound. Around the outer edge I have pleated and sewed Hamburg edging.

The inner wreath is made on a 12-inch crinkly frame, using pink starflowers, and it is then wired with fine wire to the first wreath. A description of how to make this is on page 102.

A small bow with long streamers of pink satin ribbon hangs from the bottom of the two wreaths. Against the streamers, fluffy white snow balls made from white yarn fall in a cascade. Knitting worsted was used for making the snowballs. Wind yarn around a 3-inch piece of cardboard fifty times. Slip the yarn off cardboard and tie securely in the middle with white yarn. Cut through the ends of the yarn loops and shake to fluff up. A purchased pink felt angel with gold wings hangs in the center of the wreath.

CHAPTER SIX

KITCHEN
DECORATIONS

CANDLES WITH FRUIT WREATHS
FOR KITCHEN TABLE

To CREATE the center arrangement on this table, first invert a large open wicker basket to serve as a base. Around and over this place a 16-inch flat wire frame wound with red satin ribbon. A wreath of small red spruce cones comes next; to make one, wrap a 16-inch crinkly wire frame with tape and wire the cones on. (Overlap the tip and butt of each cone about ½ inch, then wire the cone tightly to the frame.)

Invert another basket (it hardly shows in the picture) to make a base for the fat red candle in the middle. Place a 12-inch wreath of artificial fruit around this to cover the basket. If you add a few real fruits to the artificial ones, this wreath will be more attractive. Small sprays of cedar or other evergreens may be used for greenery.

The pair of small candle arrangements are made similarly, on small baskets turned upside down. Place flat red-satin-ribbon wreaths around the candles. To make a wreath frame this small, take a plate the size you want your frame to be, lay it on heavy cardboard, trace around it, and then cut it out. Measure inside the edge to make the inner circle and cut this out.

The fruits around these small candles are artificial grapes, real crabapples, and the small yellow fruits of the flowering crabapple.

PINEAPPLE KITCHEN ARRANGEMENT

The pineapple, symbol of hospitality and welcome, is a suitable decoration anywhere in the house, especially at Christmas time when we are likely to have more guests than usual. Although I use this arrangement in the kitchen, a similar one could go in almost any other room.

To preserve a pineapple, stick it with cloves. Your fingers may be a little sore after you have pushed fifty or more cloves into place, as the clove top is hard and rough, so you might use a knitting needle to make the holes in the pineapple before inserting the cloves and thus save your fingers. The odor of the pineapple mixed with the cloves is delightful and more than makes up for your trouble. A pineapple treated in this manner will dry and be everlasting. Because it will shrink to about half its original size, it is best to use a Jamaican pineapple, which is much larger than the Hawaiian. The tops of available pineapples are often rough, bent, or broken. Tucking in small pieces of greens at the top will help to cover these deficiencies and also give height and flair to the whole arrangement.

Crabapples, set in place, encircle the pineapple at the base, with white pine tucked in between.

The container is made up of a pair of Italian pottery compotes, one inverted for a base If you wish to hold these containers securely, you can put a bit of florist's

clay between them. Another method, which is a bit more permanent, is to melt some paraffin wax and pour it on the bottom of the inverted compote, and set the other on top quickly to make it adhere. The paraffin, being almost colorless, is almost invisible and can be used on many containers. When you wish to take them apart, just run hot water over.

One legend of how the pineapple became a symbol of hospitality dates to the days of sailing ships. A ship owner might instruct his captain to bring back from a voyage a number of pineapples. These were a very exotic fruit at that time. The ship owner stored them in his cold cellar or preserved them in one form or another. They were not served merely for simple Sunday suppers, but only on state occasions, to important guests. Thus the pineapple symbolized the pinnacle of hospitality. Perhaps it was also a status symbol of that particular age.

FRUIT ARRANGEMENT WITH CANDLES

The base of this simple long-lasting arrangement is a shallow basket turned upside down. Small Colorado spruce cones wired together create an interesting edge around the basket; they also hold the fruit in place. The fruits are yellow Delicious apples, yellow Bosc pears, red cherry tomato clusters, and pinkish-orange prickly pears. Scotch pine and sprigs of boxwood here and there embellish the fruits.

Small corsage-size aqua picks filled with water are very useful to hold greens in this and similar arrangements. If your greens are first well conditioned, they

will last for many days in the picks. An aqua pick has a rubber cap with a hole in the top to insert one stem. However, for a longer stem or bunch of greens, simply remove the cap.

I always pick a good-sized bagful of small tomatoes just before we expect a frost, taking green ones as well as the riper yellow and red. It is surprising how long they will last if kept cold in the bottom of the refrigerator; you can still use them at Christmas.

Short fat fruit candlesticks, cast in plaster, painted in reds, yellows, and blues, and antiqued quite heavily, are used here. (See also page 124.) Circles of red spruce cones wired together give weight and interest at the bottom.

The hand-carved wooden pheasant, finished in a reddish brown color, adds a note of dignity to this rather informal arrangement.

CHAPTER SEVEN

FAMILY ROOM

COPPER WREATH AND CONE BOARDS

YOU MIGHT wonder, looking at the abundance and variety of pine cones on the mantel, how they all stay in place without tumbling off. There is no danger, for they are all attached to two pegboards which, though hidden, hold them firmly in place. I had the boards cut in a particular length and shape (see sketch) that seemed to fit readily in many parts of the house, as well as on the mantelpiece, as you will see on the following pages.

You will need a good many cones in a large variety— old, new, small, large, fat, thin—to make a pair of cone

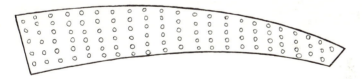

boards. Each cone is wired and attached to the peg- board separately.

Interesting effects can be achieved by cutting the cones into flower forms. The small Scotch pine cones are easily shaped with pruning shears. Starting from the top center, merely cut out as many of the scales or segments as seem necessary to make the cone assume a flower shape. Often, instead of making a sharp cut, merely cut and then tear out the scale, leaving a fringe-like edge that simulates the center of a flower.

To halve large heavy Southern or Italian pine cones, a willing helper is needed, for their tough springiness makes them difficult, if not dangerous, to cut, especially with a band saw. Following my husband's instructions:

Never try to hold a large cone with your hands while you saw it. To hold the cone safely, use two strips of ¼-inch plywood about 24 inches long by 2 inches wide. Place them on either side of the saw blade so they project about 4 inches behind the blade. Put the cone between the plywood strips lengthwise, tip toward the saw blade, and squeeze the strips together to hold the cone tightly. Now feed it against the saw teeth.

Try to keep the saw blade running on the central pith of the cone, so that you will get two even halves. If you cut a cone in this fashion, at no time will your fingers or hands be endangered by the saw blade. This instruction is very important, because cones are very tough and resilient and, unless held in some fashion such as this, could be risky to cut. The cone of the Norway spruce cut lengthwise looks most interesting and unusual.

Assemble all your cones, half cones, and cone flowers and wire them one by one. To wire cones, use thin #30 wire for small cones and heavy #24 wire for the largest ones. Hold the cone stem end down. With your other hand, slip the wire around the cone's middle, pulling it down tightly under the scales toward the base or stem end. Twist both ends of the wire firmly to secure them. Be sure you use long enough wire to have plenty left for attaching the cone to the pegboard.

Starting at the tapered end of the board with the smallest, thinnest cones, work toward the wide end

ROSES

using larger cones as you progress. Fill the interstices with small cones. Cone boards last indefinitely, are a joy to bring out each year and use in many different ways. On this mantel I have added to them sprays of white pine and cedar and copper flowers.

The two wreaths in the center are made separately. The background one is a 16-inch flat wire frame wrapped with cloth and covered with white pine (see page 6). The top wreath is a 14-inch circle of pegboard to which are wired flower forms made from thin sheet copper. This copper is quite pliable and easy to cut with heavy shears, as are thin sheets of brass and aluminum. Two or more layers of copper may be held together with ½-inch round-headed brass paper fasteners, the head of the fastener making a center for the flower. You can make roses, lilies, leaves of various shapes, numerous other flowers.

To make a rose, fasten three graduated forms together with the smallest on top. Curl the curves up more or less to simulate flower petals. To make a lily, cut a circle with a narrow wedge in it. The wedge allows you to curl one side inside the other to form the tapering cup shape of this flower.

Although this wreath has been assembled in hit-or-miss pattern, a bisymmetrical one is equally pleasing. Start, for instance, with four large forms such as roses, space them evenly, and fill in between with leaves and other smaller flower forms. Highlights and shadows on copper create a pleasing effect particularly when used against old pine panels such as this room has. If sheet metal is not available, you can use foil paper in gold or other metallic colors.

The two wreaths are wired together with #24 wire, which can also be used to hang them.

LEAVES

LILLIES

ARCH WITH STAR BASKET

This arch is formed by placing together the two wide ends of the cone boards, which are described on page 119. Here just the cones are used, without the addition of greens and flowers.

Bridging the gap at the apex of the arch is an antique brass piece. In choosing an adornment for the top, be sure it is in character and has the necessary solidity. It should not be fragile or delicate. Wired to the outside of the wickerwork star basket is our antique gold clock frame. The massive hand-carved mahogany candlesticks have small spruce cone wreaths about their bases (see pages 139-41 for directions for making wreaths).

CONES AND BELLS OVER ORGAN

Here the two cone boards described on pages 119-21, have been joined together to form an arch. To add depth and extra interest at the top, center sprigs of cedar have been added. The catalpa tree pods, dangling at the ends, are a rich shiny brown and have large fat seeds in them which give added texture. As these pods dry, they twist and turn in fascinating curves, and almost resemble tassels.

The wicker bells have openwork that you can run ribbon through. Large satin bows join the arch and the bells together, contrasting with the soft natural textures. With a golden-brown wormy chestnut wall as a background, you might use ribbons of rich dark brown, bright, gay red, or yellow-green. Any of these colors will be particularly effective if your candles match your ribbon. If you have trouble finding chartreuse-colored candles, buy yellow ones, and give them a thin coat of green oil paint, letting some of the yellow show through. I have not found that this kind of paint creates any hazard when the candles are burned.

GARLAND AND STAR BASKET
OVER ORGAN

The decorations in this picture have been shown and explained in detail in other pictures. However, this is an example of how the same basic decorative elements may be combined with others to effect many different compositions. It is surprising how many of these ornaments may be hung in several alternate ways and be just as attractive.

When the garland was used on the front door, (page 33) it was hung with the ends up. Here it is turned around the other way, and small sprays of yew have been tucked into the top of the styrofoam. Brown satin ribbon twisted like ribbon candy was hairpinned to the bottom edge of the styrofoam.

The star basket is detailed on page 134. The Della Robbia candlesticks were encircled with small wreaths of yew in this arrangement, to tie in with the yew added to the decoration above.

CLOTHESPIN WREATH OVER ORGAN

It takes a box and a half (or about 40) old-fashioned wooden clothespins to make this wreath. As a base for the pins, use a circle of plywood or, if it is to be used only indoors, heavy cardboard will do. The clothespins should be glued on. Before you start, divide the circle into four equal parts. Lay the clothespins on one section to judge how they should spread before you start to glue them on. The heads of the pins should touch, and the pins fan out. Place each pin so that both legs show, as in the photo. Glue on only a few, then put a weight on top of them until they set; an iron or a brick will do for weighting.

This wreath is equally interesting on the wrong side. It has a nice flat surface where another wreath of a completely different character could be hung. A fruit wreath, for instance, is charming.

A dark cedar wreath made on a 16-inch flat frame makes a perfect background for the clothespins. Here, the inner circle has been filled with a round Christmas picture glued on cardboard. A green satin bow bridges the space between the organ and the wreath, relating the wall decoration to the organ. The combination of cedar and yew on the wall sconces and again on the small wreaths around the candles on the organ brackets also tends to bring this entire wall area together.

CARVED DELLA ROBBIA WREATH
AND ESPALIERED TREE

This is a simple but effective arrangement to fill a wall space above a small table. At Christmas time I often take down the pictures and mirrors that we live with the year round and replace them with Christmas motifs. This one includes a hand-carved Della Robbia wreath painted in a medley of browns, yellows, tawny reds, and soft blue. The white pine wreath used for a background is made on a 16-inch flat wire frame.

The espaliered apple tree frame and tub here are made of metal, but you might make an espalier tree by using the wire frames that are available at many nurseries or garden equipment stores. First wrap the frame with brown florist's tape. This gives the effect of branches and also keeps wires from slipping when leaves and fruit are wired on. Fill an ice-cream carton of the right size with either paraffin wax or plaster of Paris. Plunge the frame into this mixture and hold steady until it hardens. Just before it hardens, cover the top of the wax or plaster with peat moss. Paint the outside of the carton to simulate a tub. Wire on real or artificial leaves and fruits. I have used white pine and andromeda leaves, which most closely simulate apple leaves and were available in good condition, and wired them to the frame with fine (#30) wire.

To give better balance to the whole composition, I have upturned a small brown basket for a base under the espalier tree. The little brown-leather-bound book and the old brown tin box are accessories in keeping with the whole design.

The Della Robbia wreath shown on page 136 could be used in place of the carved one.

TREE TABLE AND WALL ARRANGEMENT

Trees, an important element in Christmas decorations, can be made in many possible shapes and sizes, and of many different materials.

Plywood, Masonite, or any wallboard makes excellent bases for any of the trees on the wall here. Draw the tree, trunk, and pot all in one piece and jig saw it out.

Left to right, the first tree on the wall is decked with green artificial roping from the five-and-ten-cent store. Staple one end of the roping on the back at the bottom, then wrap it across the front, staple again on the back, and cut. Repeat, working up the tree and being sure to pull the roping tightly so that it does not slip. You could make a tree in the same way using real evergreen roping.

Wind red Christmas bead strings across the tree at intervals. I put a silver plastic star on the top to match the few strands of silver that came mixed in with the artificial green roping. These decorations are found on most Christmas ornament counters.

Pad the front of the tub with cotton before covering it with red velvet, to give it a third dimension. A band of green satin ribbon finishes it nicely.

The second tree is made much the same way as the first, except that the materials—moss fringe and satin ribbon—are different. Moss fringe in a wide variety of colors is available at curtain and upholstery trimming counters. Wind this tree first with red satin ribbon, then teal-blue moss fringe in regularly spaced lines.

For the tree trunk and tub, glue on felt—brown for the trunk and red for the tub. A small red and brass bell decorates the top.

The third tree is covered with light blue felt. Glue it on, making sure to cover the edges (it is not necessary to cover the back.) Use bands of light yellow-green moss fringe here, with tiny jingle bells. (Sew or wire the bells to the fringe before you glue it across the tree.) Cover the trunk with dark brown felt, the tub with red felt bordered by a band of darker red fringe. The star at the top is red felt. These young gay colors are admirably suited for a child's room.

The two trees on the table are made on styrofoam bases. The first is cone shaped, and is trimmed with a rather odd combination of materials—buff-colored moss fringe and tiny hemlock cones. Secure the fringe at the bottom of the cone with a heavy wire hairpin, then spiral it to the top, leaving even spaces for the row of hemlock cones. Secure the fringe at the top with another hairpin. Select the tiniest cones you can find, and, using a pencil end, make a small indentation in the styrofoam for each one. Dip the butt end of the cone in glue and press firmly in place in the styrofoam. Continue upward in a spiral row, placing the cones as close together as possible. I have glued little arbor-vitae seeds between the cones on my tree.

Naturally it is best to set this tree in its tub *before* you decorate it. The tub is a small, squat tin can with wide brown satin ribbon glued on. Place the styrofoam cone on top of the tin, bear down quite heavily, and twist back and forth a bit to make a groove in the styrofoam to hold it in place.

A black oriental teakwood base, ordinarily used for flower vases, gives solidity and interest. Under it is a cardboard wreath wound with brown satin ribbon to complete this little tree's rather elegant look.

The last tree is feminine and delicate, suitable for a lady's bedroom or bath. The soft green pottery container is filled by a piece of styrofoam; the dowel stick trunk is topped by a ball of styrofoam. Push the dowel into the ball ½-inch or so to make a hole; dip the dowel in glue, push it into the hole. Repeat for the container filling. Cover the styrofoam ball with sheet moss attached with heavy wire hairpins. Glue more sheet moss over the styrofoam in the pot. The artificial pale pink rosebuds have strong enough stems to stick into the styrofoam. A brown velvet ribbon glued around the container, and a brown-stained wooden base, finish the bottom.

The small ornaments at the bottom of the picture can also be used on a real Christmas tree. The base is made from cardboard tubes; the ones we find inside wax paper, foil paper, wrapping paper and so forth. Cut with sharp heavy scissors a length of tube the width of your ribbon. The tube will squash a little while you are cutting but it will straighten out again. Glue the ribbon to the tube. Using silver tinsel, wind around the middle of the tube and make a loop at the top by which to hang it. A jingle bell was wired to the bottom. These are unusual and attractive ornaments. They can be made in all one color or in many different ones.

The cardboard tubes also make large Christmas candles. They may be painted or covered with paper. Cut a circle of styrofoam about 2 inches long to fit tightly in the top of the tube. Using the stub of an old candle not more than 1 inch long, cut a circle in the middle of the styrofoam and insert the candle. Let the candle burn until the styrofoam is lightly covered.

STAR BASKET MADONNA

This favorite star-shaped basket has been used in a number of arrangements in this book, but each time in a somewhat different way. Here, a circle of cardboard was cut to fit inside the basket. Then a colored Madonna picture clipped from a magazine was glued on.

To make the wreath that encircles the Madonna, select as many cones of the same size as is necessary for the size wreath you want. Norway spruce cones are especially pleasant to use. If the cones are dry and not pliable, soak them in warm water overnight. When using cones this size, you don't need a wire frame; simply wire the tip of one cone against the butt of another. Fine #30 wire is strong enough to hold them. The cones should overlap each other by about 1 inch. Pull the wire tightly under the scales and twist up firmly in the back of two overlapped cones, thus joining them together. Repeat until the wreath reaches the desired size.

The wheat is tied with ribbon that is gold on one side and orange-red on the other. This can usually be obtained through florists. In summer when you are preparing garden corn for dinner, save the husks to make flowers. After you have pulled the husks back from the ear, break off the corncob, leaving a few kernels of corn on the stump of cob. Cut the ends of the husks in rounded petal form, and arrange them; set the "flowers" aside to dry and they will be ready to use by Christmas.

These three pieces would also be interesting over a fireplace that has no mantel.

The arrangement below them is based on two more baskets. One is a very old one, and the other is modern. The modern one, which I have turned upside down to form a base for the other, matches perfectly the color of the corn-husk flowers and the wheat. The old basket has a metal rim around the top, latticed straw sides, and a bottom of brown-painted tin. Atop this, I have placed a wreath of artificial fruits, which I made on a crinkle ring wrapped with tape. I wired the fruits on in small bunches with fine wire. Often I set a few real fruits among the artificial fruits. Any small tomatoes (cherry or plum) are perfect for this. Also a few greens will give variety.

DELLA ROBBIA WREATH

The Della Robbia family flourished in Italy for over a hundred years during the fifteenth and sixteenth centuries. Celebrated sculptors and ceramists, the family became noted, among other things, for their creations of sculptured and glazed ceramic wreaths of fruit and flowers in color. These wreaths were of evenly balanced sections. Today, wreaths of similar nature and arrangement, whether of living or other materials, are called "Della Robbia."

In all the years I have been creating Christmas decorations and of all the styles and kinds I have made, the Della Robbia wreath is my favorite. To me, the combination of fruits and flowers is unsurpassable.

Looking at a completed wreath you might think it would be difficult to make, but, as with most handmade things, time and patience and a few instructions are the main requirements.

The fruits, flowers, berries, and other materials in this wreath are: green crabapples, green grapes, two varieties of yellow crabapples ("Katherine" and "Dorothea"), Scotch pine cones, yellow strawflowers, blue starflowers, and leaves and seed pods of andromeda (Pieris).

Remember to pick or buy crabapples in the fall before the first frost and store them, for they will not be available at Christmas time. There are two methods for keeping crabapples fresh. The first one is very simple: Merely put them in a plastic bag and keep them in the refrigerator. Go over them every two weeks to eliminate any bad ones. The other method is to dip each apple quickly into hot, hot paraffin wax. This seals the apple, and it is more likely to last longer. Be sure that the wax is *really* hot when you dip the apples, otherwise, you get a thick, unpleasing coat of paraffin wax on them. Even after the apples are coated they must be kept cold. It is wise to dip even the small crabapples. Pick any and all of the flowering crab fruits you can get your hands on—yours, your neighbors', any willing friend. If you don't pick them, the frost will get them.

The basis of the wreath is a 12-inch flat wire frame wrapped with cloth and with yew tucked into the folds. A Della Robbia wreath is usually made up of even sections—four, six, or eight units. For a 12-inch wreath, four units are sufficient.

Assemble your fruits and flowers, making sure you have enough of everything you will need. Start placing the largest fruits first. (In the wreath shown it was the green crabapples.) The blossom end of an apple has always been more interesting to me than the stem end, so I put this facing out, and secure the apple as follows:

Cut a piece of heavy wire long enough to go around the wreath. Force the wire through the middle of the apple. Place the apple in position on the wreath. Adjust the wires so that they are hidden in the yew. Bring the two ends of the wire together in the back of the wreath, and twist them up tightly. Put all four apples on at even intervals in this fashion.

Large yellow strawflowers with a heavy wire stem already attached can be bought at florist's shops. Place the flower on the wreath, insert the wire under the yew and up the other side, making a loop. Then twist the end of the wire around the stem up near the blossom.

The small light blue starflowers are everlastings grown in Italy and are available dyed many different colors. A Della Robbia nearly always has some blue in it, and these little flowers seem to be just perfect. Make small bunches of them, using fine wire to hold the stems. Leave about ½ inch of wire extending from the bunch, to be thrust into the apples. With their stems cut short, the flowers are so light that the wire in the apple holds them securely in place. If you do not wish to wire them to an apple, you can wire the bunch to a toothpick and thrust it into the folds in the fabric along with the yew. Either of these methods may also be used for the small crabapples.

Attach the grapes by placing a piece of fine wire across the stems and in between the yew, finally twisting it up tightly in the back. Do not use heavy wire or the bunches will snap. Fine wire is strong enough to hold the grapes without breaking the stems.

The pine cones can also be wired to toothpicks and

tucked into the fabric folds. Cut the andromeda with stems long enough to insert similarly into the folds.

Tie a length of ribbon at the top for hanging it and the wreath is finished. You can make wreaths similar to this up to three weeks before Christmas, keeping them outdoors covered with newspapers and a carton over them to protect them from the frost, or hanging them in a cold garage. The carton will protect them from the birds and a few mothballs placed near them will protect them from mice.

The background wreath shown in the picture is a 16-inch flat wire frame wrapped with a soft gray-blue cotton cloth. Over this is wound a copper "ribbon," leaving spaces of the blue fabric showing between the eight bands of copper. The copper "ribbon" is a Chore Girl designed for scrubbing pots and pans (see page 52). The satin ribbon holding the Della Robbia wreath and the blue-and-copper wreath together is a shaded color ranging from yellow on one side of the ribbon to orange with tinges of red. This is a ribbon I use quite frequently as it blends with and complements most any combination of fruits.

THREE HERITAGE WREATHS

Heritage wreaths, so called because it is anticipated they will be passed on to future generations, are made of such substantial and lasting materials as nuts, cones, and seed pods. You can collect cones and seed pods for Heritage wreaths wherever you find them—new ones and old gray weathered ones alike—in the woods, at garden centers, anywhere. You may prefer to use only

new cones to make a shiny wreath, but often various
shades of gray and brown are most pleasing together.
I use no finish whatsoever, but if you prefer, you can
spray the wreath with clear plastic spray or varnish it
with a clear varnish.

Most Heritage wreaths are made on wire frames, to
which each cone is wired separately. I used to make
mine that way too, but now I find it much easier to
work with a styrofoam wreath and secure the cones
with Elmer's glue. First back a 16-inch styrofoam wreath
with heavy cardboard, as there will be quite a bit of
weight to your finished wreath. Lay on your large white

pine or Norway spruce cones evenly spaced around the wreath. It is difficult to force these into the styrofoam, so it is best to put a large blob of glue on the styrofoam. Use wire at both ends of the cone to force it firmly against the bed of glue and hold it fast. Leaving it in place overnight will insure good adhesion; then you can remove the wire. I attach these temporary wires as follows: Pass a long length (about 12 inches) of fine wire under the styrofoam, and bring the ends up on both sides of the part of the wreath where the cone is placed. Run the wire over the tip end of the cone about 1 inch down. Bring the two wires together and twist them tightly. Repeat, wiring the butt end of the cone. Long cones are the only ones that need to be wired in this way.

To attach a smaller cone, force it into the styrofoam to make a bed or pocket, then lift it out, add some glue, and force the cone back into its pocket in the styrofoam again. Hold it in place for a short time. All the smaller cones can be glued without wires.

The entire wreath should be studded with cones. Some may be cut in the flower forms described on page 14. As the picture shows, materials placed at different angles will create visual interest. When you have completed the entire wreath once, go over it again with very small cones and seed pods. I love to use little poppy seed pods, gluing them on top of cones already in place to build up a third dimension. Don't forget the edges; achieving a rounded edge is easier when a styrofoam wreath base is used.

Here the large wreath is hung over the shield of a copper sconce from which the candle brackets have been removed. The small wreaths are hung over the tops of copper sconces.

FRUIT STONE AND FIR WREATH

The use of peach stones in this wreath was inspired by my husband's wood carvings. He had just finished carving a Della Robbia wreath which I was admiring. I was enjoying a peach, just picked from my garden, and as I finished the peach, for the first time in my life I *looked* at the stone. "Why it is just like a little carving!" I exclaimed. From then on I saved all our peach stones, and before long it occurred to me to consider other fruit stones. I thought the smooth coats of prune pits would make a lovely contrast with the rough-textured peach pits; similarly the little smooth, round stones of cherries. I decided to save all of them. Even though I washed them as clean as possible, some of them turned black with mildew. These I simply immersed in pure Clorox bleach, let them bubble and fizz for a few minutes, then washed them in clear water. This worked—they were clean again.

A circular styrofoam frame was the base for this wreath, backed up with heavy cardboard because of the weight of the stones. A circle of cardboard, cut slightly smaller than the wreath and glued on with Elmer's glue, formed the backing.

When you begin your own wreath, try positioning the stones in various patterns until you find what suits you best. Be sure the base is lying flat on a strong table, for you must use pressure on it to make a little bed or pocket for each stone. Force the end of the stone into the styrofoam; don't be afraid to push quite hard and wiggle it a little as you are pushing. After you make the bed in the styrofoam, put in a few drops of glue and then set in the stone.

Be sure to place stones at an angle. Do not have them standing up straight like soldiers, but on a slant. The peach stones go in first, in trios: the center one straight ahead, the other rows fanning outward in each direction. Then glue on the prune stones, and last the little cherry pits. The cherry pits do not go into the styrofoam but are glued in place on top of the other stones. Do not try to complete the wreath at one sitting. Do one section at a time and let it dry; then do another section.

The stones in my wreath have not been sprayed, varnished, or coated with any finish at all. They have acquired their own natural beautiful patina.

In this photograph, the wreath has been wired to a basket that has a lovely circular pattern in the center. The color of the basket blends with the natural color of the stones. A flat wire frame filled with fir was used for the background wreath; Scotch pine, yew, cedar, or juniper could be used.

FRUIT STONE AND RIBBON WREATH

This is the same peach-prune-and-cherry-stone wreath as shown on page 142. Merely by a change of background, a quite different effect is created.

Here, a 16-inch flat wire frame wrapped with white-dotted green satin ribbon backs up the peach wreath, which hangs freely on top of the ribbon wreath. There is no need to wire the two together when they are used indoors. A full, abundant bow with long flat streamers finishes the composition.

Brown satin ribbon would also be effective against a pine or chestnut wall, soft green or blue velvet against a painted wall.

TRIPLE WREATH
OF NATURAL MATERIALS

Three separate wreaths are used in this decoration. The outer wreath was made of pepper weed in mid-summer. This is a good time to make many decorations and avoid the rush in December. Also many materials are best gathered then. The pepper weed is light green and very full in early summer; if you wait too long, all the seed pods will fall off. Use a crinkly ring for the base, first wrapping it with florist's tape. Attach small bunches of pepper weed with fine wire, being sure to overlap each bunch about one-half its length. The tex-

ture of pepper weed is very soft and lacy, and the light green color will fade to a lovely pale buff as it dries.

The second wreath is made of dried brown magnolia leaves, as described on page 41.

The third wreath is the most fun to make. All the material of which it consists is usually thrown away, so the cost of this wreath is merely in terms of styrofoam, glue, time, and patience. There are: date stones, two sizes of olive pits, and watermelon seeds. None of these need be bleached, merely soaked and washed clean. Glue them on a styrofoam base in any desired pattern.

Heavy wire is attached to the back of each wreath. They all hang separately.

I used an old piece of weathered pine to hold the fat candles that flank the ceramic Holy Family.

PEACH STONE AND CRABAPPLE WREATH

An unusual combination of materials was used in making this wreath—peach stones, hemlock cones, and crabapples.

First, three rows of peach stones were glued onto a 16-inch styrofoam wreath. Between the stones, small hemlock cones were glued. The completed wreath was then glued to a large, 18-inch circle of unfinished mahogany-faced plywood.

It often adds interest to fill in the center of a wreath with a different color or texture. For this one, the shield of a copper sconce is used. It is not highly polished, since I prefer copper to be soft and mellow, especially when used in this manner.

To finish the mahogany circle, small red crabapples

were wired to a princess pine roping. Be sure to buy or gather your crabapples in September when they are available. It is difficult to find them at Christmas time. They will keep very well in your refrigerator.

On either side of the mantel shelf are heavy oblong pieces of unfinished mahogany, on top of which I have placed short fat candles. Candles of this size, called household candles and available only in white, may be found in five-and-ten-cent stores. You can antique them slightly with a little burnt sienna oil paint mixed with turpentine and a little varnish. In front of the mahogany blocks, red apples alternate with white pine cones.

PEACH STONE WREATH WITH ANGEL

The basic wreath is the same as shown on page 147, made of peach stones and tiny hemlock cones. However, something else has been added to the inside circle: the burrs of the copper beech. They are a lovely dark brown on the outside with an interesting rough texture. The insides are buff in color, soft, smooth—almost fur-like in feeling. I merely thrust the stems into the edge of the styrofoam base. Use glue if you want them to remain in place permanently.

Princess pine roping hangs over the top of the wreath, draping down the side, to frame the tall hand-carved angel and set off the brass candlesticks. Either a Madonna or a pair of choir boys would be appropriate in place of the angel.

CRÈCHE

The placement and surroundings of a crèche are of great importance. Instead of merely setting it on a table in the usual manner, consider making a special place for it. One way is to remove one or two shelves of a bookcase to give a feeling of depth and dimension, and to frame it as shown here.

An old tin lantern was used to simulate the stable. There are holders for two candles, but they do not show in the picture. Its handle is hidden by the branch of box-wood on the right. The glass across the front has been removed and the chimney on top is concealed by the straw "thatch," which came originally already woven to-

gether as wrapping for a bottle of champagne. It makes a perfect top for the stable. The inside of the lantern is painted a soft gray-blue.

Three levels have been created to give interest and dimension to the scene. The first level is the book shelf. The second is formed by what I call a "rhythm board," which I designed many years ago. This board is uneven in outline, giving a feeling of rhythm and motion. It is hand-carved on the edges and painted an earthy color. A rhythm board can be used as a base for fruit and flower arrangements, but, when used with the crèche, serves as the earth level. The third level is, of course, the stable.

The tree on the left is a branch of euonymus. The tree on the right is boxwood. These are secured by pin holders anchored to the board with florist's clay. Bits of scattered straw soften the picture and knit the elements together.

The placement of the figures can itself tell a story. It is more usual to have all the figures facing toward the baby. However, I like to create the feeling that not all the people have arrived. The wise man at left is still in the distance with his hand shading his eyes as he searches. The shepherd boy at right appears to be coming up the hill because he is placed back of all the other figures on the first level. Actually, this placement came about because both legs had been broken off the shepherd accidentally, but we like the effect of depth this creates. The cow is placed as if coming around the corner of the stable, with one eye on her calf. The horse and sheep have seen the baby and stand in awe. The goat has not yet come near the stable, but the two older sheep are bowing before the Holy Family, while the little lamb lies down in the midst of everything and gazes outward.

SWINGING, RINGING TREE

This Christmas tree hangs gracefully by its tip from a beam in the family room, eliminating the problem of trying to conceal a Christmas tree stand. Such a hanging tree can be a great boon to the parents of small children. Busy little hands either cannot reach the branches, or, should they tug at them, there is no danger of the tree toppling over.

Long brass pipe chimes are attached to a screw eye set into the butt of the tree trunk. A long wide red ribbon, tied to the bottom of the tree trunk just where the chimes are attached, enables you to sit on the divan in front of the fireplace and pull the ribbon to "swing and ring" the tree.

In selecting a tree, proportion is very important. Keep in mind the height of the ceiling and the size of the room. Don't be afraid to cut the tree down a bit, if necessary, when you get it home. All too often a Christmas tree can seem to overpower everything else in a room. Comparatively speaking, our tree is always small—usually 4 to 5 feet tall—although the room is rather large.

To decorate the tree, we have over the years used such materials as red and green crabapples, dried Chinese lanterns, fruits, stars made from wheat stems, various-sized spools of thread, different sized bells, evergreen cones sprayed copper or gold, dried starfish sprayed gold, and simple shapes of colored paper. All these ornaments were tied to the tree with red ribbon.

Here the tree is decorated with various-sized starfish and red crabapples. The starfish were gathered last summer and presented to me, a few at a time, by a four-year-old granddaughter. These were laid flat on a long board

and placed in the sun to dry. This took most all summer. Just before they became thoroughly dry, I pierced the tip of each one, using a large needle and nylon thread, and made a loop to hang it by. When they were dry we sprayed them gold.

CHAPTER EIGHT

DECORATIONS
FOR CHILDREN

SANTA

Looking at the commercial Santa masks available a few years ago, I could find none that appealed to me, so I went about making one myself. Here's how to make him.

Fill a 12-inch pie plate with cotton batting, padding with a few extra layers where the cheeks will be. Cut a piece of an old sheet large enough to cover the front of the pie plate, allowing enough for it eventually to meet and be sewed together in the back. Next, tack the piece of sheeting to any flat surface, lay the pie plate on the sheet, and draw around it.

Now draw a twinkly-eyed jolly Santa, with crayons. It might be wise to practice on another piece of sheeting first. Old sheeting has a very soft texture. Use the crayons lightly to make a Santa with a soft, kind, gentle face. The eyes are important and should be accentuated. Don't forget his round red nose and pink cheeks. Because the mouth is covered with a mustache and whiskers, it is not necessary to draw it. When you have made his face to your liking, lay the sheet over the cotton-filled pie plate, adjust it to fit, and sew it up in the back.

Santa's hat can be made of red Indian Head cotton or cotton flannel, or, if you want a more dressy Santa, you can even use red velvet and trim it with ermine! Cut a triangular piece of red material wide enough to go around the pie plate and as long as you want the cap to be. Seam to make a cone shape. Now try it on. Make any adjustments needed, then hand sew all around the head, stitching through the sheeting and into the cotton batting stuffing. The fur around his hat is pure white surgical cotton right out of the box. Cut a piece about 5 inches wide, long enough to go all the way around, and hand sew it on. The pompom is another piece of cotton cut and shaped into a ball, then sewn on.

Now for Santa's whiskers. They are spun glass, so be sure to wear gloves when handling this material for it is very fine and can work into your skin. Buy four or five boxes of spun glass "angel hair," either plain or wavy, at Christmas decorations counters. Sew a spun glass beard on his face, simply stitching over and over to hold it in place. Sew the mustache on going from side to side, and don't forget to twist the ends. Be prepared to trim Santa's mustache and whiskers next year; they may "grow" quite a bit for, as Santa hangs, the spun glass stretches longer and longer. Your Santa will probably not start with whiskers as long as the picture shows—it has taken years to grow these beautiful long whiskers.

Santa is very rugged and can withstand a lot of real winter weather, as his whiskers fly beautifully in the wind.

CHILDREN'S CHRISTMAS TABLE

In our house, the children usually have their own table for Christmas dinner, with their own table cloth, dishes, and decorations. This seems to make everybody happy. Of

course, decorations are a part of the delight for both children and parents.

One year we made these cut-out wooden Christmas trees, which are very easy to store. We drew the outline of tree, star, and tub on ¼-inch plywood, then cut two at a time with a jig saw. We made a slot in one of the trees extending from the top to exactly half-way down, and a slot in the other tree that starts at the bottom and extends half-way up. This allows the trees to fit together, making them demountable. The tree with the slot in the top is nailed onto a 2½-inch plywood square.

The small trees are about 5 inches high, made singly and glued on a base. All are painted dark green with bright red tubs and have gold stars at the top. Each child has his own tree.

For the arrangement pictured, I placed a small round basket upside down on a lazy Susan in the center of the table and set the large tree on top of the basket. Small angels playing musical instruments (purchased at Christmas decorations counters) stand around the edge of the lazy Susan and in front of each small tree. Various-sized jingle bells from the five-and-ten-cent store hang on each branch of the large tree by a fine wire run through the top of the bell, the ends twisted together into a loop; these are Scotch-taped in place on the branches.

ARCH AND DRUM

The arch with the middle drop is a very easy decoration to make. And by merely changing the drop, you can produce an entirely different decoration.

For the base, use a wire coat hanger. Press the ends

together and bend downward to form an arch below the
hook (see page 12). Almost any evergreen will be suitable for this arch.

Cut two pieces of the evergreen long enough to reach
from the middle of the hanger to below the bottom of
each side. Sometimes it is necessary to use more than
one piece of greenery to make it full enough. Use heavy
wire at the top where the branch is thicker, but fine wire
will do for wiring the middle and the end. Be sure to
wire on a sprig or two at the top to cover the hook.

The drum and the horns can be found in the five-and-
ten-cent store. Red baubles cover the top, and the entire

decoration hangs from a long satin ribbon. Spray-on snow adds the finishing touch.

Some other ideas for drops: A string of pine cones, a string of pepper berries, satin or glass baubles of various sizes, or a string of sleigh bells left the natural metal or painted white with sprigs of holly wired at intervals along the leather strap. I have used 3-inch purple satin ribbon effectively also, making loops at the top and letting the ends of the ribbon hang down. Wire a cluster of blue-green and purple baubles at the top under the loops, and half-way down wire a smaller bunch. Or try any other combination of colors.

PINE CONE CHRISTMAS TREE

The inspiration of this small Christmas tree came from the large cone of a Southern pine. Its shape is exactly

like a tree, and by simply tucking sprigs of greenery between its scales, you can easily make a tree. The secret of
a well proportioned tree lies in the choice of evergreens:
cedar and boxwood are the best. Their needles and leaves
are small and fine, perfect in scale for your tree. Children
love to make these.

A fully opened pine cone will stand by itself and needs
no holder (at left in the picture). First, select a sprig
about 4 or 5 inches long that looks like the top of a tree
and push it into the top of the cone as far as possible.
Then fasten it securely in place with fine wire.

Now start at the bottom, using full bushy sprigs; tuck
them firmly between the scales all around the cone. They
should be about 5 inches long or whatever length will
balance best with the top. Work around and up the cone,
using shorter lengths of sprigs as you approach the top.
It may seem amazing that greens will stay in the cone although they are merely pushed in, but they really do.
Many times I have traveled some distance with one of
these little trees and very seldom had to replace any
greens.

The center cone in the picture, shown partly decked
with greens, is Italian. I bought a whole bale of them at
a flower market; they were so beautiful I just couldn't
resist them. They were not fully opened and would not
stand alone, so to open them, I placed them in a warm
oven. (The odor of pine was delightful throughout the
whole house, but the pitch on the bottom of the oven!)
Even after they were removed from the oven they had to
have holders. A small red glass vigil light was perfect for a
cone tree in many ways. Shaped like a tub, it was Christmas red; I needed only to light the candle and let it burn
until enough wax had melted to hold the bottom of the
cone. When I set it in, the hardening wax held it firmly

in place. Then I filled it out with sprigs of greenery as detailed above.

Many kinds of decorations are suitable if they are of proper proportions. Christmas tree bead strings are excellent. Remove the beads from the string, and make stems of heavy wire for one or two at a time. Be sure to cut the wire stems different lengths, so you can use long stems at the bottom of the tree and shorter ones at the top. Just push these stems in between the greens.

The cone tree at right stands on a very simple base: a circle of painted wood with four short pieces of dowel glued on for legs, resting on a small cardboard wreath wrapped with red satin ribbon.

Pairs of these trees are charming on a mantel or coffee table, on an hors d'oeuvres tray, or on a small dining table. In the dining room, small green grapes make an unusual decoration: Thread a colored sequin on a common pin and stick it into one end of a grape. A toothpick stem on the other end can be thrust into the tree. For children's trees, small lollypops or gumdrops on toothpicks are excellent decorations.

WREATH, BELL, AND
TABLE DECORATIONS

Children will be able to make these, and adults may enjoy trying their hand at them too.

The outer wall wreath is a 16-inch flat wire frame wrapped with cloth strips and covered with evergreens, (see pages 5-6). Next is a 12-inch flat wire frame wrapped with red ribbon. Boys who are interested might cut the circle out of plywood instead. However, both circle frame and star may be cut from heavy cardboard and covered with paper or painted gold, silver, or copper. Cut them to fit the basket you plan to use in the center. The basket can be wired top and bottom to the ribbon wreath with fine wire. A piece of fine wire Scotch-taped to the

back of the star at the top secures it to the basket. This would be a most suitable design to use in back of a crèche. Be sure to make it in proportion to the figures used.

The bell on the ribbon is cardboard covered with tiny hemlock cones. Glue them on vertically, close together in even rows as far down as the place at which the bell begins to flare out. Weight the cones with a brick or a pressing iron until they are firmly stuck to the cardboard. Cover the lower part of the bell with a thin coat of glue. The cones in final rows are glued at the base with their tops facing outward. This makes them project farther than the flat rows, giving contour to the bell. The clapper is a large cone with a fine wire wrapped around the butt, of a length long enough to be Scotch-taped to the back of the bell. The small red ribbon bow at the top is also wrapped with a fine wire, again leaving a length long enough to glue to the back of the bell. The wide ribbon is also glued to the back. This little bell fits nicely in the middle of a paneled door.

The decorated match boxes of wooden matches are excellent Christmas gifts and are especially good for children to make. Place a match box on green construction paper or other decorative paper, trace around it, and cut out carefully on the lines. Coat the box lightly with glue and apply the paper front and back, being sure not to cover the sides used for striking. Next, with heavy green wrapping cord, form a circle a little smaller than the box cover; glue it to the box. To the middle of a length of narrow red ribbon, wire three or four of the tiniest hemlock cones you can find. Tie the ribbon in a single knot to cover the wire, then glue the ribbon to the box at the spot where the cord joins. Cut the ends of the ribbon.

The other match box is red paper covered with a narrow strip of gold paper glued to the top and bottom. On the front of the box, trace around a quarter (this will act as a guide for the circle which will be the inside edge of the wreath). Make a Heritage wreath, using the tiniest cones, seeds, and berries you can find, gluing them on around the circle. The seed pods of the Japanese andromeda are excellent—small, rugged, with an interesting texture. Also attractive are the tiny cones of the black alder—in fact, these are the tiniest and most rugged I know of. Let children look at these small seeds and cones through a magnifying glass to enjoy their elaborate detail and design.

Empty thread spools with red satin ribbon glued around the middle can be embellished by seeds of Japanese andromeda. Glue them around the base of the spool and encircle the birthday cake candle which fits in the hole. These can serve as place card holders for a children's or adult Christmas table.

The next two decorations are foolproof and therefore especially suitable for children to make. The bases used can be of many different things—small pie plates, biscuit tins, large jar tops, or, as in the picture, a typewriter ribbon dispenser for the large one and a small instant coffee jar lid for the smaller. Select enough even-sized cones to fit around the inside of the containers. Scotch pine cones are a good size for larger candle holders, red spruce for smaller ones. Choose greens to match the bases in size and proportion.

Now for the candles in the centers. For a hospital bedside table, a vigil light is perfect. A small candle, a miniature choir boy or Santa candle for the young, a large or fat candle for a simple Christmasy effect, or a tall slender Madonna candle to give a reverent atmosphere—there are many candles for many different effects.

Assemble all your materials, making certain that they all fit. Put paraffin or short stubs of used candles on the stove to melt. Fill the containers three-quarters full of the melted wax. Just before the wax sets, place your centerpiece and then the cones around it. Now tuck the evergreens in between each cone. The hardening wax holds everything in place. For bases under the larger decoration, a green glass lamp base sits on top of a circle of cardboard covered with red ribbon. The smaller decoration is nice to use for individual place settings, or on meal trays for invalids or hospital patients.

CHAPTER NINE

DECORATIONS FOR THE BIRDS

BIRDHOUSE

THIS BIRDHOUSE has year-round tenants. The copper roof and the little brass cherub blowing his horn on top were once a part of an elaborate chandelier and because of their materials, take the weather very well.

On the four sides underneath hang seed bells, trimmed with bright red ribbons and sprigs of yew for a gay Christmasy look. The birds surely seemed to appreciate these festive handouts.

At the base of the birdhouse is a large birdbath. It is deep enough for the larger birds to enjoy, but a large flat stone placed in the birdbath enables smaller birds to use it as well. A brass lawn sprinkler is used as a fountain at the base of the pole; since the pipe is attached to the outside hose outlet, the size of the spray can be easily adjusted. It can be turned just high enough to fill the birdbath or really high in order to water the roses which in summer surround the birdbath.

PINE TREE WITH POPCORN
AND CRABAPPLES

In our yard stands a small white pine growing in a pot and pruned once a year to keep it in proportion. Because of the pruning, it has become quite dense and bushy, and it is a year-round joy in the garden.

It makes a perfect Christmas tree for the birds. We string circles of popcorn on fine wire and hang them here and there. We also wire on crabapples, and pine cones with either suet or peanut butter pushed between their scales.

When the snow is deep, I place a small box of sand under the branches on top of the pot, to make sure the birds will have gravel as well as seed. The feeder above the tree, which holds seeds, is painted purple; a bow of red and a sprig of yew wired to the top give it a Christmasy air.

ESPALIERED PEACH

My espaliered peach tree, though still rather small, makes a dramatic point at the end of the brick path that passes between the vegetable and cutting gardens. We can see it

from the family room all winter long. It needed a bit of color for Christmas, so I wired on fat red apples for the birds to enjoy, and they really did enjoy them—I had to replace the apples a number of times. The uncluttered branches were convenient for them to perch upon while pecking away at the apples.

APPENDIX

THERE are many suppliers throughout the country who offer fine selections of materials, accessories, and mechanical aids for the gardener and the arranger. There are others who may specialize in certain types of materials. It is not possible for me to know or enumerate all of them. I suggest that you check your own area for a source of supply. But if you are unable to obtain your needs locally, here are a few suppliers with whom I am familiar.

DOROTHY BIDDLE
10 Broadway
Hawthorne, New York

> *A well-known supplier who can take care of almost any garden need.*

THE GARDEN SPOT
170 Washington Street
Marblehead, Massachusetts

> *Noted for its comprehensive inventory of all types of materials needed for the making of Christmas decorations. All kinds of frames and bases, including the basket type, are available, plus a wide variety of dried pods, cones, nuts, leaves, and an excellent choice of better fruits and flowers.*

MRS. JOHN BURNHAM
Blue Mussel
Naples, Florida

> *All kinds of sea shells.*

The following firms specialize in a wide variety of dried materials.

ST. GERMAINE'S FLOWERS
P. O. Box 1795
Stockton, California

> *Cones, weeds, dried and preserved pods. Heritage wreath kits.*

JACK SULLIVAN'S
4000 Broadway
Everett, Washington

> *Dried materials gathered from all sections of the United States.*

BOTANICAL BOUNTIES
Box 70
Palm Springs, California

CAMPBELL'S
1914 Tenth Street
Brementon, Washington

DRUHE'S
Box 36
Carmel Valley, California

THE DRIFTWOOD STUDIO
1139 North 25th Street
Billings, Montana